EVALUATING THE IMPACT OF LEADERSHIP DEVELOPMENT

A Professional Guide

Center for
Creative Leadership

leadership. learning. life.

The Center for Creative Leadership is an international, nonprofit educational institution founded in 1970 to advance the understanding, practice, and development of leadership for the benefit of society worldwide. As a part of this mission, it publishes books and reports that aim to contribute to a general process of inquiry and understanding in which ideas related to leadership are raised, exchanged, and evaluated. The ideas presented in its publications are those of the author or authors.

The Center thanks you for supporting its work through the purchase of this volume. If you have comments, suggestions, or questions about any CCL Press publication, please contact the Director of Publications at the address given below.

Center for Creative Leadership
Post Office Box 26300
Greensboro, North Carolina 27438-6300
Telephone 336 288 7210
www.ccl.org

Jennifer Martineau
Kelly Hannum

EVALUATING THE IMPACT OF LEADERSHIP DEVELOPMENT
A Professional Guide

CENTER FOR CREATIVE LEADERSHIP
Greensboro, North Carolina

CCL Stock No. 187
©2004 Center for Creative Leadership

Published by CCL Press
Martin Wilcox, Director of Publications
Peter Scisco, Editor, CCL Press
Karen Mayworth, Associate Editor
Sylvia Graham-Shoulberg, Copy Editor
Joanne Ferguson, Production Editor

Cover design by Joanne Ferguson

Library of Congress Cataloging-in-Publication Data

Martineau, Jennifer.
    Evaluating the impact of leadership development : a professional guide /
by Jennifer Martineau and Kelly Hannum.
       p. cm.
    ISBN 1-882197-76-3
    1. Leadership—Evaluation. 2. Executives—Training of—Evaluation.
I. Hannum, Kelly. II. Title.

HD57.7.M39257 2004
658.4'092—dc21
                                                    2003046188

CONTENTS

PREFACE

The Center for Creative Leadership (CCL) has conducted evaluations of its programs, products, and services for more than twenty-five years. It evaluates new and revised programs for quality and to answer specific questions (such as the point at which specific behaviors begin to show meaningful change). CCL also evaluates client-specific initiatives to determine the impact of leadership development on individuals, teams, organizations, and their communities.

The principles that guide CCL's evaluation work are confidentiality and accuracy. CCL takes every possible measure to protect the confidentiality of individual participants when it is sharing their evaluation data—in aggregate forms—with others (such as their organizations), and it strives to provide accurate and complete information about the success (or failure) of a development initiative with all key stakeholders. CCL follows the guidelines set forth by the American Evaluation Association and the American Psychological Association.

What CCL has learned from these many years of evaluating leadership development programs doesn't just sit in its organizational library or in an intranet database. Because its mission is to advance the understanding, practice, and development of leadership, CCL intentionally shares its learning with a broad range of interested professionals who are active in the practicing fields of leadership development and evaluation; academic fields such as psychology, education, and sociology; and organizational fields where leadership development becomes a strategic implement.

In its evaluation work CCL uses many tools that it has developed over the years by drawing on best practices and research from inside and outside CCL. Each approach it takes to evaluation depends on the specific expected outcomes for a development initiative. The tools and approaches we share in this book are the result of CCL's intentionally evaluating its work with individual and organizational clients. It's our expectation and our hope that this book will add to the available information about evaluation tools targeted specifically to leadership development initiatives.

We envisioned this publication as a way to educate and assist others in the evaluation process. Therefore, we have combined basic education about evaluation with examples of evaluation design processes and tools. This information gives individuals with or without evaluation training, but with some behavioral sciences knowledge or experience in the organizational development field, an understanding of what it takes to design, implement, report on, and use evaluation studies regarding the impact of leadership development on individuals, groups, and organizations. We have tried to present a broad array of tools and processes from which readers can choose when designing and conducting their own evaluations.

The framework we introduce and use in this book is flexible enough to meet many needs. For example, evaluators can use it before designing leadership development tools. They can use the processes described here to build evaluation into the development intervention itself so that it becomes an integrated method of determining its progress and success. Even if an organization requests an evaluation after an intervention has been completed, the tools and processes in this book can help evaluators design useful and relevant oversight.

We envisioned an audience for this book comprising a broad group of people: those on the front lines of leadership development who want to enhance their practice and/or gather evidence to demonstrate the value of their work. This group can include human resources managers, consultants, nonprofit groups that conduct leadership development training, scholars, managers, and employees with leadership development responsibilities.

Much of our work is collaborative, and thus there are more people who have contributed to this work than we could possibly name. However, there are a few individuals without whose contribution this book would not have been a reality. Bart Craig, Chuck Palus, Hallie Preskill, Sharon Rogolsky, and Ellen Van Velsor—we owe a great deal to you for "playing along with us" at various times on this work. This is as much a product of your thinking and practice as it is of ours.

We are also grateful to our reviewers and the editorial staff who provided us with additional perspectives that allowed us to create a better final version. We extend our thanks to Joanne Ferguson, Sylvia Graham-Shoulberg, Karen Mayworth, Brenda McManigle, Hallie Preskill, Peter Scisco, Ellen Van Velsor, Wynne Whyman, and Meena Wilson.

Finally, and most important, our ability to have the experiences necessary to create this book rests on the support, encouragement, and understanding of our family and friends. Jennifer especially thanks her parents, Herbert and Ellen Wells, for placing a high value on education and hard work, and her husband, Jim Martineau, for his undying patience with her love of her work. Kelly would like to thank her parents, Elizabeth and Wallace Hannum, as well as her siblings—Rebecca Rogers, Bryan Rogers, and Wallace Hannum—for their love.

INTRODUCTION

Scratch the surface of any successful organization, and you'll likely find systems designed to evaluate how well it runs. A constant drive for efficiency, productivity, and stewardship of resources pushes commercial and not-for-profit organizations to weigh options, balance trade-offs, and make better decisions about internal processes, customer relations, product releases and distribution, new programs and services, and other issues. An evaluation system gives organizations a logical and practical framework for collecting and assimilating information.

The approach to evaluation we present in these pages can be applied in a variety of contexts, but our focus in this book is the evaluation of leadership development initiatives. Although many professionals do difficult and excellent work in and with organizations to build leadership capacity, tools for supporting the evaluation of leadership development are few and far between. Our expertise in this area is coupled with a responsibility to share what we've learned. Our experience evaluating leadership development initiatives has given us specific ideas for how that work should be conceived and conducted: that it should be participatory, be integrated with initiative design, and enhance organizational learning.

Using a participatory approach means involving key stakeholders—people inside and outside the organization who are, or will be, affected by the initiative being evaluated and/or by the outcomes of the evaluation itself. If lessons from an evaluation are to be successfully applied in an organization, all relevant stakeholders must be involved in the planning or informed about the goals and objectives of both the initiative and the evaluation. As much as possible, they should also be involved in the interpretation of results and the creation of action plans based on the results because this ensures that the evaluation takes into account their perspectives and will secure their endorsement of the results and the plans that arise from them.

Ideally, the focus and design of an evaluation are tightly integrated with the design of the initiative it evaluates. Both activities require a targeted discussion of the intended impact of the initiative. When collaborative processes are used to focus the evaluation and to apply the results and evaluation work is integrated into the design and implementation of an initiative, both the initiative and the evaluation are more effective, and organizational learning can result.

That learning is reflected in the organization's increased knowledge regarding barriers to and facilitators of organizational change. In identifying how and where an initiative has been successful (or not), stakeholders can learn what organizational processes, structures, areas, or systems support change as a result of the organization's development initiatives, as well as what may need attention to be most effective. In addition, roles and responsibilities are further clarified during the evaluation planning process. That process also includes strategies for sharing results and lessons across the organization.

New products and services and effective strategies can keep an organization at the front of the pack, but effective leadership development initiatives will ensure that it can create the capabilities that will allow it to stay in the race no matter what changes occur or crises arise. Evaluation helps people in organizations meet several goals. It helps them make informed decisions about how to improve development initiatives and helps them examine the degree to which development goals have been accomplished and what work remains to be done. If development outcomes aren't met, evaluation helps people in organizations understand the problem, learn from their experiences, and apply those lessons to improving individual, team, and organizational performance. These characteristics make an evaluation system not only important but also necessary for individual and organizational success.

1

THE CYCLICAL NATURE OF THE EVALUATION PROCESS

Developmental initiatives, when well designed and carried out, link different kinds of learning opportunities and occur over a period of time. They also link back to the organization so that individual development is connected to organizational goals in a cycle of assessment, practice, and learning. We would argue that the results of such initiatives are best measured with an evaluation process that is itself cyclical—not isolated in its methods or defined by discrete points in time. Recognizing the cyclical nature of evaluations allows organizations to use them as planning and learning tools that augment the individual and group impact of leadership development.

Change is the norm for many organizations, and evaluation can be a tool for enhancing and dispersing organizational learning amid what can be seen as continuous transition. This approach creates a fluid process for evaluating leadership development initiatives while enhancing individual, group, and organizational learning, rather than creating a measurement system designed solely to create valid results (Preskill & Torres, 1999). CCL has based its framework on that approach, with some modifications in terminology to reflect its focus on leadership development.

The first phase of our framework, focusing the evaluation, includes learning and planning activities that guide evaluators and others toward results that are relevant and beneficial (see chapter 2). Activities that focus an evaluation include the following: identifying stakeholders for the initiative and for the evaluation, determining the purpose of the initiative and the evaluation, identifying the resources available, determining the level and type of impact, surfacing expectations, and drafting evaluation questions and potential data-collection methods. Ideally, evaluators conduct these activities in conjunction with the design or implementation of the initiative. The complexity of organizational contexts and cultures combined with the complexity of developing leaders requires processes to help stakeholders develop a common understanding of issues, purposes, and roles. Combining the design phases of the evaluation and the initiative helps ensure the utility and efficiency of both processes. As you focus your evaluation project, this combination will help you ask the appropriate people the right questions. At the end of this phase, you will have developed your evaluation strategy.

Once the focusing activities are complete, the next phase is designing and conducting the evaluation, covered in chapter 3. In this phase evaluators and key stakeholders design and apply the evaluation plan. Measuring and interpreting degrees of change are complex endeavors. It's at this stage that you will address research design considerations such as using multiple data-collection techniques. To manage the evaluation project's complexity, you can use the information stakeholders have provided during the focusing stage to explore the benefits, drawbacks, and caveats associated with different evaluation techniques.

The final phase in the cycle, using evaluation findings (see chapter 4), is often overlooked. Typically, the results of the evaluation are compiled and reported by the evaluation team, which includes evaluators and key stakeholders (supporters, staff, and participants, for example), and this team may also make preliminary recommendations for action. But our position is that organizational learning is the ultimate goal of a well-conceived and professionally produced evaluation. Delivering a report with recommended actions isn't enough to realize that goal. Implementing and monitoring the action plan that arises from your evaluation help ensure that such learning will take place.

2
FOCUSING THE EVALUATION

The ideal time to plan an evaluation is when the development initiative is being designed. When the planning is integrated in this fashion, evaluation questions can be used to design the development initiative so that it will be likely to promote the desired results. This is an effective way to focus your evaluation on stakeholder expectations. However, it's not always possible to design an evaluation during the design of the initiative. Often organizations don't realize the need for an evaluation until after conducting a development initiative.

In designing a focused evaluation, it's also important to understand the ebb and flow of work in the organization and to take critical times in an organization's calendar into account. Many organizations have periods in their annual cycle that are particularly busy and stressful—bad times for evaluation activities. For example, if the people you wish to collect survey data from are enmeshed in annual budget planning, they may not have time to complete your survey. Making the evaluation process as simple and convenient as possible can ameliorate scheduling problems and help you gather the information you need.

Whether you can design your evaluation in unison with the creation of the development initiative or you must design it after participants complete the process, it's essential to define the key elements of your evaluation design. The following actions can help you successfully gather and focus the information you will need to design an effective evaluation.

- Identify stakeholders. *Who will be affected by the development initiative and its evaluation?*

- Define purpose. *What are the reasons behind the development initiative?*
- Determine resources. *Are there sufficient resources—money, time, and staff—to support the evaluation?*
- Establish the desired types of impact. *Is the development initiative expected to have an impact on individuals, groups, or the organization?*
- Establish the period of time over which the impact is expected to occur. *Is the development initiative expected to have short-term, midrange, or long-term impact?*
- Surface expectations. *What is anticipated to occur as a result of the development initiative and its evaluation?*
- Determine evaluation questions. *How can stakeholder expectations be reflected in the evaluation questions being used?*

Identify Stakeholders

Stakeholders are people inside and outside the organization who are, or will be, affected by the initiative being evaluated and/or by the outcomes of the evaluation itself. If they do not get their questions answered, it's unlikely that your evaluation will serve its purpose, no matter how rigorous your design. To avoid this disappointment and waste of resources, it's important to identify and include stakeholders early in the evaluation design process.

Make all of your stakeholders aware that evaluation usually creates a demand for change—in individuals, in organizational systems, and in the initiatives on which it is focused. It's important to have widespread agreement that stakeholder groups will use the findings of the evaluation to implement constructive change. Use "Focusing the Evaluation: Stakeholder Identification Worksheet" on page 7 to identify the key players in the design and evaluation of the development initiative.

Focusing the Evaluation: Stakeholder Identification Worksheet

List and describe the stakeholders in the organization who are involved in the development initiative or have an interest in the outcome of its evaluation. In identifying stakeholder position or description, go beyond titles to include such people as the designers of the initiative, trainers, human resources staff, potential participants, senior managers concerned with the results, managers whose staff will participate in the initiative, and the groups funding the initiative. In identifying stakeholder interest, make notes about the particular information needs your stakeholders have with regard to this initiative and evaluation. This list of questions isn't exhaustive but offers guidance. If your circumstances suggest other questions, substitute them for these, or add them to this list.

Who has an interest in the development initiative?
Name:
Stakeholder position/description:
Stakeholder interest:

Who has an interest in the evaluation's processes and results?
Name:
Stakeholder position/description:
Stakeholder interest:

Are there additional people whose support is required for the success of the initiative or the evaluation?
Name:
Stakeholder position/description:
Stakeholder interest:

Who has decision-making authority with respect to both the initiative and the evaluation?
Name:
Stakeholder position/description:
Stakeholder interest:

Define Purpose

Effective leadership education initiatives often link several different kinds of developmental opportunities and occur over time rather than as a single event. They also link back to the organization so that individual development is connected to organizational goals. Typical learning opportunities in such initiatives might include an assessment-for-development initiative, one-on-one coaching, skills-based training, challenging assignments, and action-learning projects (see "What It All Means" on page 9 for definitions of these components).

The purpose of a development initiative may seem to be clear, but it's important as you focus your evaluation to confirm that stakeholders have a shared understanding of that purpose. Designing the development initiative and its evaluation at the same time is an effective way to ensure that stakeholders have that understanding. Defining how your evaluation will measure the impact of the development initiative puts abstract goals ("We will develop better leaders") into practical terms ("Our senior managers will understand how to give feedback to their direct reports"). Using multiple perspectives to confirm stakeholder assumptions will help you better define the purpose of the initiative so you can design a more effective evaluation. Although not all stakeholders will participate in determining the scope or focus of the evaluation, it's important that you understand all of the assumptions the stakeholder group holds about the purposes of the development initiative. A thorough understanding of how elements of the development initiative fit together and the context in which the initiative and evaluation will take place are crucial to focusing your evaluation.

In reviewing the leadership development initiative, evaluators can gain a full picture of the process by investigating several different avenues. "Focusing the Evaluation: Purpose Definition Worksheet" on pages 10–11 can be helpful in directing your review.

What It All Means

action-learning project—a collaborative inquiry process in which participants work and reflect on real problems with learning partners, producing a tangible outcome while at the same time learning from the experience.

assessment-for-development initiative—an initiative in which data from assessments (usually including assessment instruments) are used to help participants identify their strengths and determine where they need further development. The assessment information in these initiatives is almost always used exclusively for development purposes and not administrative purposes (such as promotion or salary decisions). This type of initiative is intended to help participants assess current skills and behaviors, increase self-awareness, change perspective, and clarify values and goals.

challenging assignments—assignments that provide opportunities for individuals to learn and/or apply skills in a manner that would not be possible as part of their normal work responsibilities.

one-on-one coaching—a formal developmental relationship through which the participant engages in a series of one-on-one feedback sessions with a coach (the coach can be a person from his or her organization or someone outside the organization). Coaches can play a variety of roles, such as feedback provider, sounding board, feedback interpreter, and others.

skills-based training—a development experience in which individuals gain knowledge and practice behaviors necessary to hone present skills or develop new ones. The purpose of this type of training is to improve performance in a specified skill area.

Focusing the Evaluation: Purpose Definition Worksheet

Seek answers to these questions from the initiative's key stakeholders before designing your evaluation plan. The answers will help you define what stakeholders see as the purpose of the organization's development initiative. With that information you can focus your evaluation to measure expected results.

What specific business challenge does the organization hope to address by setting up this initiative?

How does this initiative support the organization's business strategy?

What specific leadership needs does this initiative address?

What are the purposes of the leadership development intervention(s)? For example, are stakeholders generally content with the status quo of the organization's leadership but seeking a standard of leadership practice? Do stakeholders want a program of development in order to create and reinforce a new and different set of skills?

Are there any other external and internal pressures or demands for creating this initiative?

Will participants be held accountable for their development as a result of this initiative? If so, how?

What level of accomplishment is the initiative intended to promote? Knowledge acquisition? Awareness change? Behavioral change? Skill development? Performance improvement?

What type of impact is the initiative expected to have? Will it affect only individuals? Will it affect teams or groups? Will it have broad organizational impact?

How will the information in the initiative be delivered and over what span of time? Will it be a single five-day session or two three-day sessions held six months apart? Will it include one-on-one coaching components?

What data will be collected during the initiative that may be useful in an evaluation? What data are being collected by other groups or departments that may be useful in an evaluation?

What evaluation techniques are already in place for the initiative?

What assessment instruments will the initiative use that could also be used to measure change during the evaluation?

What kind of information about the impact of the initiative do various stakeholders need? What will they do with the information? Why do they need it?

Determine Resources

To design an effective, focused evaluation, you will need to know what resources (money, time, and staff) are available. Evaluations typically take up 5 percent to 20 percent of the cost of a development initiative. As a general rule, the cost of the evaluation depends on the complexity of the initiative and the evaluation. The following are important questions to ask: When are stakeholders expecting to see results? What skilled staff members are available to perform the evaluation? How much data will be collected during the evaluation? How will the organization use the evaluation results?

Depending on when stakeholders want to see evaluation results, for example, you will need to make resources available to collect the necessary data, analyze it, and communicate the results. If stakeholders want to measure results at multiple stages, you will need to allocate your resources appropriately to meet that need. Skill sets you will want to tap for conducting an evaluation include database experience, statistical knowledge, survey development, interviewing experience, and project management. If the organization has available staff with these skills, that can reduce costs.

Types of Impact

Organizations evaluate their systems and processes to determine whether performance expectations have been met. When it comes to leadership development initiatives, organizations frequently expect a demonstrable return on investment, but they don't often define what they mean by that. Stakeholders assume that development initiatives will affect the individuals who participate, the groups or teams to which they belong, and the organization as a whole. But they may not expect impact at all levels (individual, group or team, and organization) for every initiative. Understanding the type of impact the initiative is intended to have and the type of impact stakeholders expect it to have can strengthen your evaluation design by clarifying the goals you will measure against. Your evaluation design is stronger and more apt to provide relevant results when it focuses on stated goals and expectations.

According to the figure below, this could mean that

- individuals will be better able to perform their leadership roles in the organization,

- groups may be better able to perform effectively in the organization,

- the organization may experience an improvement in climate and/or in the bottom line.

Expectations for Leadership Development

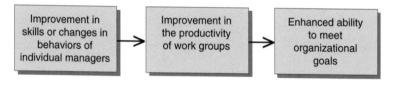

Source: McCauley, Moxley, & Van Velsor (1998).

Individual-level impact. A leadership development initiative should have an impact on the individuals who experience it. The impact itself, however, can vary. For example, individuals may learn new leadership models and practices, or they may learn new business- or organization-specific practices. Participants may develop an increased awareness of their personal managerial style and how it affects others. They might also change work-related behaviors or increase their productivity using newly acquired skills. Impact will vary depending on the content and design of the initiative and the development needs of individual participants.

For example, three- to five-day assessment-for-development initiatives are likely to result in participants' acquiring critical knowledge, building awareness, and gaining some ability to apply lessons to certain behaviors and situations. For changes to become ingrained in an individual's performance, additional developmental experiences, such as one-on-one coaching and challenging assignments, are necessary. Challenging assignments provide the opportunity for individuals to learn and apply skills in a manner that is not possible as part of their normal work responsibilities.

Team- or group-level impact. Development initiatives created for individual leaders can also have an impact at the team or group level. For example, a manager's local group might perform more effectively after that manager has enhanced his or her leadership capability. It may be able to get products to market more quickly because its manager has developed skill in focusing group effort. After participating in a development initiative and learning skills that encourage better communication among team members, a team leader may be able to manage the team toward more effectively supporting team and organizational goals. When development initiatives are targeted at intact teams, outcomes are more pronounced and more quickly observable because the team as a whole is able to put the members' new awareness, knowledge, and skills into practice immediately.

Organization-level impact. When organizations invest substantial resources in developing leadership capacity, they look for results that will help them achieve strategic objectives, sustain their effectiveness, and maintain their competitive position. The quality of an organization's leadership is only one contributing factor to reaching those goals. Even so, a leadership development initiative can, among other things, facilitate culture change, enhance the organizational climate, improve the company's bottom line, and build a stronger, more influential organizational profile when all leaders in the organization have participated in it. An organization may also use development initiatives to augment the internal branding of the company name, as is the case when a company offers development opportunities to present itself as an appealing place to work. With regard to evaluation, stakeholders will want to gather information that provides evidence of the link between leadership development and measures of organizational success.

Impact over Time

If the impact of an initiative is expected to occur over a period of time, you can design your measurements to account for short-term, midrange, and long-term impact. Design your evaluation plan and choose your measurement and reporting methods to address each of these time frames.

The short-term impact of a development initiative can include what participants think about the initiative and their experience with it immediately after completion. Short-term impact also includes the development of new ideas or new self-awareness based on what participants have recently learned from their developmental experience.

To measure midrange impact, the evaluation should occur three to six months after the development initiative ends. Measurements at this time usually relate to individual skill improvement, behavioral change, or team development. Assessing a development initiative's long-term impact occurs nine months to a year (or more) after the initiative ends. Areas that benefit most from this type of evaluation include performance improvement, the attainment of more complex skills, and organization-level change.

Surface Expectations

An organization often conducts evaluations to determine whether its expectations have been met. As previously mentioned, the usual expectation is that there will be a demonstrable return on investment. But there are often additional expectations that may be explicit or implicit in an organization's investing resources in development. Failing to understand and address those expectations can have negative consequences for the initiative and its evaluation.

Some common expectations for leadership development initiatives are that participants will become better leaders and will share a common language of leadership (for example, they will learn and be able to put into practice specific leadership terms, models, and styles) so that they will understand how to work with each other more effectively. Organizations may also expect it to be easier to find and retain talented employees because developmental opportunities exist. Other expectations include making the organization a more engaging place to work, delivering products or services to market and to clients more quickly, and increasing revenue in the case of for-profit companies or broadening and deepening impact in the case of not-for-profit organizations.

A development initiative designed to meet objectives is linked closely to stakeholder expectations. If you integrate the design of your evaluation with the design of the initiative, you will be measuring the right results. Part of that integration process is linking your evaluation plan to stakeholder expectations. Use "Focusing the Evaluation: Surface Expectations Worksheet" on pages 17–18 to specify implicit and explicit expectations so that you can take them into account during the design phase.

Determine Evaluation Questions

Once you understand the expectations of all key stakeholders for both the development initiative and its evaluation, you can

Focusing the Evaluation: Surface Expectations Worksheet

If you integrate the design of your evaluation with the design of the initiative, you will be measuring the right results. Part of that integration process is linking your evaluation plan to stakeholder expectations. Use this worksheet to specify implicit and explicit expectations so that you can take them into account during the design phase.

What specific outcomes have stakeholders said they expect in order to consider the initiative a success?

Identify specific behaviors that stakeholders expect participants to exhibit as a result of this initiative.

How are these behaviors different from or similar to current behaviors being exhibited?

Is there baseline information about the group's current behavior? (Review previous assessment activities, if available.)

What are the implications of not pursuing a development initiative or an evaluation?

Over what period of time is the initiative to occur?

When do stakeholders expect the initiative to have its desired impact (how much time will they allow before they expect to see the desired change)?

What questions will stakeholders and others ask about the effective-ness of the evaluation?

What evidence of impact will the stakeholders consider necessary to believe that the intended outcomes have been achieved? What type of data will they accept (qualitative or quantitative)? What sources will they trust (for example, participants, their managers, customers)?

How do stakeholders expect results to be communicated (final evaluation report, update memos, etc.)?

define the questions the evaluation should answer. It's important to understand the difference between evaluation questions, which define a broad but intentional direction, and survey questions, which are created specifically to generate data for analysis. Evaluation questions should be well defined and linked specifically to clear objectives. The questions should be informed by stakeholder expectations so that they appropriately address those specific concerns. If the questions are not linked to stakeholder expectations or are otherwise unclear, you may come up with data that you can't interpret or communicate with respect to the goals set out in the development initiative.

Evaluations frequently are designed to answer multiple questions. However, we recommend that your evaluation address only a few key questions to keep the evaluation goals clear and to maintain a focused effort during the implementation stage. The questions in "Focusing the Evaluation: Developing Evaluation Questions Worksheet" on page 20 will help you determine and define questions to use in your evaluation.

Developing questions using the aforementioned worksheet as a guide, several specific questions related to a particular development initiative can be investigated. Those questions might include the following:

- To what extent does the leadership development initiative meet its stated objectives?

- Are there any unintended benefits or challenges raised by the initiative?

- To what degree are participants prepared to apply what they have learned to their work?

- To what degree have participants applied what they have learned to their work?

Focusing the Evaluation:
Developing Evaluation Questions Worksheet

Your evaluation should address only a few key questions to keep the evaluation goals clear and to maintain a focused effort during the implementation stage. Use this worksheet to determine and define questions to use in your evaluation.

What are the critical questions the evaluation should answer?

From whose perspective are the questions being posed?

When are answers to those questions expected?

What are the objectives of the development initiative?

What aspects of the initiative address those objectives?

What logical connections can be made (or should be investigated) between initiative outcomes and the intended impact?

What types of impact and what time frame are of interest to stakeholders?

What outcomes are possible to measure, given the timing of the evaluation in relation to the implementation of the initiative?

What elements of organizational context are important to understand?

How will the information from the evaluation be used?

- To what extent have participants made significant behavioral changes?

- What is the impact of participants' behavioral changes (or other changes) on those around them?

- Has the organization experienced the intended changes (benefits) as a result of the initiative?

Target population. The outcomes of a leadership development initiative depend heavily on the individuals involved. The skills and perspectives that they bring to the initiative and the context in which they work affect what they are able to learn and the results they are able to achieve. Therefore, it's critically important for you to fully understand the target group for the development initiative you are evaluating. "Developing Evaluation Questions: Target Population Worksheet" on pages 22–23 can be helpful in determining the target population, identifying what those individuals bring to the development process, and specifying how best to measure the results of that process.

Managers of the target population. Because the success of a development initiative is affected by its organizational context, evaluators should become familiar with the managers to whom participants report. The managers' support and involvement have an impact on participants' ability to effectively integrate what they've learned and apply the skills they've acquired. "Developing Evaluation Questions: Managers of the Target Population" on page 24 can be helpful in defining the managers who are likely to be most affected by the development initiative and what role they might play in the initiative.

Developing Evaluation Questions: Target Population Worksheet

It's critically important to fully understand the target group for the development initiative you're evaluating. Use this worksheet to determine the target population, identify what those individuals bring to the development process, and specify how best to measure the results of the process.

Who is the target population for this initiative (for example, shop floor supervisors at all manufacturing locations)?

Why do these individuals need a development initiative? Why does this initiative focus on them in particular?

What type of training or development has this group experienced in the past? What has their reaction been? What has been the impact of prior training and development?

How do the participants view this particular initiative? What positive and negative associations does it have from their perspective?

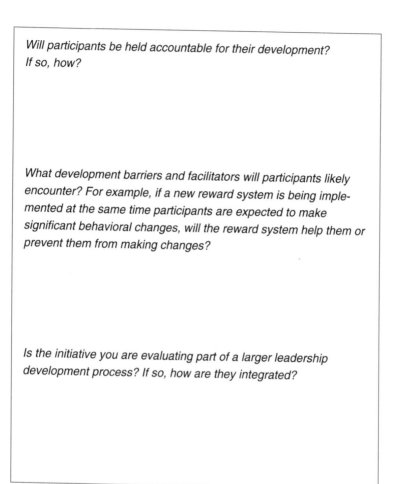

*Will participants be held accountable for their development?
If so, how?*

*What development barriers and facilitators will participants likely
encounter? For example, if a new reward system is being implemented at the same time participants are expected to make
significant behavioral changes, will the reward system help them or
prevent them from making changes?*

*Is the initiative you are evaluating part of a larger leadership
development process? If so, how are they integrated?*

Final Steps: Identifying the Sample and Choosing a Data-Collection Method

As you prepare to match your evaluation questions with data-collection strategies, consider which groups of people are likely to have the information you need to answer your questions. Reviewing your list of stakeholders can help you target the appropriate people for data collection. You may want to collect data from an

Developing Evaluation Questions:
Managers of the Target Population

Because the success of a development initiative is affected by its organizational context, evaluators should become familiar with the managers to whom participants report. Use this worksheet to define the managers who are likely to be most affected by the development initiative and what role they might play in the initiative.

To whom do the participants report? Who are their managers?

How might managers of participants be oriented to the development process? For example, will the organization provide a letter explaining the process, defining expectations, and outlining the type of support that's needed and expected?

Will participants' managers be responsible for pre- and post-intervention coaching related to participants' ongoing development? What type of support might the managers of participants need in order to be effective? Are they getting that support?

Will participants' managers be held accountable for participants' ongoing development? If so, how?

How might the managers hinder participants' development efforts or the outcomes of the initiative?

entire group, or you may want to collect data from a sample. For example, information about the trainers' behavior in the classroom may best be collected from participants because other stakeholder groups are unlikely to have direct information about that experience. Conversely, participants may not have detailed information about such matters as the relationship of organizational HR policies to leadership development success. The complexity of your evaluation questions might also influence your choice of sample respondents. For example, are there multiple perspectives that you need to capture from a diverse group of stakeholders?

Another question to ask when identifying your sample is, What group will be able to provide credible information and maximize the use of the evaluation results? For example, if your evaluation questions are designed primarily to inform the organization's executive team and you know that the executive team does not find the XYZ group a credible source of information, it will be important for you to get information from another group instead of or in addition to the XYZ group. It's difficult to achieve this level of knowledge about an organization's political underpinnings, so you may have to invest time in earning the trust of stakeholder groups.

When it comes to selecting a data-collection method, keep in mind that no single method (survey, interview, observation, or assessment instrument, for example) can fully tap the opinions and experiences of respondents. Therefore, the most effective evaluations use more than one method. This allows the strengths of one method to compensate for the weaknesses of another—what's called *data triangulation*. The more important, complex, and/or potentially controversial an aspect of the evaluation is, the more data and types of data may be needed to respond to stakeholder expectations.

Data are either qualitative or quantitative. Depending on your audience and the type of information you need, one or the other may be more appropriate. In many situations, combining qualitative and quantitative data can provide powerful evidence for understanding and demonstrating impact. You must also consider the resources available to you for the data-collection and analysis stages of your evaluation.

The following questions illuminate inherent strengths of different data-collection approaches. During the design of your evaluation, use them to guide your thinking about the possible approaches you might take. Select those collection methods that have the best chance of getting the information you need to carry out an effective evaluation. (More detailed information about specific data-collection techniques can be found in chapter 3.)

Which methods are best suited for answering your evaluation questions? If your question asks how often or how much, a quantitative approach (such as a survey or an assessment instrument that gathers frequencies or percentages) would be appropriate. But if your question asks in what ways or how, a qualitative approach (such as face-to-face interviews or focus groups) might be a more effective collection method.

What is the purpose of your evaluation? How will the information be used? The answers to questions defining purpose and use provide insights into the kinds of information needed. For example, individual stories (qualitative data) serve a very different purpose than the frequency of instances or aggregated performance scores (quantitative data). Stories may provide rich context and meaning, while aggregated performance data give a sense of the pervasiveness of impact. Think about the stakeholder group with whom you will share the data. What kind of evidence will be credible or persuasive with them? Knowing your audience may help you determine that one method is more appropriate than another. Because different kinds of data lead to different kinds of understanding, it's important for you to think about how useful certain kinds of data will be as stakeholders look toward putting results into action. But be careful not to allow the preference of the stakeholder group to determine how you collect your data. The methods you choose should always be appropriate for the question.

What motivated the need to evaluate in the first place? If the goal of your evaluation is to gather information from a range of individuals, a quantitative method (such as a survey) might be the most efficient and cost-effective method. But if the purpose is to understand the complexities of a situation (to get more in-depth information), qualitative methods such as face-to-face interviews or focus groups are more effective.

How practical and feasible is each method? If you must conduct your evaluation quickly and assess a large number of people using limited resources, it might be best to use a quantitative method such as a survey or assessment instrument. If you have enough time and resources (both technological and human), you can reasonably choose from qualitative methods such as observation, telephone and face-to-face interviews, and focus groups. In addition to financial resources and time constraints, give careful consideration to the practicality and feasibility of using different approaches given the evaluation expertise available to you (data collection, management, analysis, and interpretation). For instance, if you plan to use interviewing as one of your data-collection techniques, how will you analyze that information? If you plan to collect survey data, how will you present the results?

Creating an evaluation plan that links your evaluation questions with your data-collection techniques (see "Evaluation Plan Design Example" on page 41 in chapter 3) is a useful strategy for developing a comprehensive and well-documented evaluation plan. Although it takes additional effort at the beginning of the evaluation project, it typically saves time (as well as confusion and disappointment) in the long run.

A Plan to Use Evaluation Results

An organization doesn't conduct training programs without expecting participants to use what they've learned. Likewise, your evaluation won't be worth much if its results are not used. Organizations and evaluators need to work together with key stakeholders to achieve the most effective use of the results. Understanding and making explicit the purposes and benefits of evaluation can facilitate that process. Information from evaluations can, and should, be used to enhance organizational learning. You can help organizations with this task by planning how you will communicate the results of the evaluation and how the organization can use those results in strategic ways. (Read more about the use of evaluation results in chapter 4.) As you focus your evaluation, consider how you can measure and communicate information about a development initiative's impact so that the organization and the initiative's designers can use the results in a meaningful way—to gain deeper knowledge of process and systems, to pass on to the greater organization the lessons participants have learned, and to design more effective development opportunities.

Focusing the Evaluation: A Checklist

☑ Plan your evaluation when the development initiative is being designed.

☑ Identify stakeholders with an interest in the initiative and its evaluation.

☑ Define the purpose of the evaluation.

☑ Determine what resources are available for conducting the evaluation.

☑ Establish the types of impact the development initiative is expected to have.

☑ Establish the period of time over which the impact is expected to occur.

☑ Surface expectations about the development initiative and its evaluation.

☑ Determine evaluation questions.

☑ Identify the development initiative's target population.

☑ Identify the managers of people in the target population.

☑ Identify the sample and choose a method for collecting evaluation data.

☑ Make a plan for using the results of the evaluation.

3
DESIGNING AND CONDUCTING THE EVALUATION

After you have focused the evaluation in its intent, you and the key stakeholders are ready to design it and carry it out. To do this, you will select the specific evaluation methods you will use, customize those methods to meet the specific demands of your evaluation plan, and then implement them. To help you make those selections and guide your implementation, the following evaluation design guidelines provide tactics and tips regarding the measurement of change.

Evaluation Design Guidelines

Follow these evaluation design guidelines whenever possible in designing your evaluation. They will help you improve the quality of the evidence you collect and present—making it more difficult for others to dismiss evaluation findings as an anomaly or the result of some measurement fluke or design flaw. Following these guidelines does not guarantee defensible results, but it does improve the likelihood that you can gather and present powerful evidence of impact. Additional guidance is provided by the Joint Committee on Standards for Educational Evaluation (1994).

Examine impact from multiple perspectives. Different stakeholder groups have different perspectives on the impact of a development initiative. When evaluating skill levels at the start of the process and in evaluating how much an individual has changed at the end of the process, directors, board members, and program staff, for example, differ from each other and from participants themselves. Although for some purposes one perspective might be considered more relevant than others, evaluators should consider all perspectives, since getting the whole picture is one of the most important elements in designing a valid evaluation. Consider who has the opportunity to directly observe or experience the type of changes you want to assess, and ensure that you collect appropriate data from those individuals.

Assess the different kinds of change that can be observed. Developing leadership capacity often involves multiple types of change (for example, new knowledge that brings enhanced self-awareness and prompts skill development), so understanding where an intervention may be having an impact and where it may be falling short of expectations is critical to designing an effective evaluation. Because individuals are ready for different kinds of learning or change at different times, it's important that you design your evaluation to capture change as it occurs. Observable changes can include knowledge and awareness gains, individual behavioral change, individual or group performance improvement, and changes in the organization.

Use multiple data-collection methods. No data-collection method is perfect. Each has its benefits and shortcomings. An evaluation design that uses multiple methods can reveal information about all of the different kinds of impact stakeholders expect and can provide you with the most comprehensive sense of what kinds of change are occurring. For example, behavioral change might be best captured by a 360-degree instrument designed to measure change, but face-to-face interviews may be the best way to understand the obstacles people face in implementing desired behavioral changes. End-of-initiative evaluation surveys might be the best way to measure participants' immediate satisfaction with a training initiative, but they don't reveal issues of individual development in the way that questionnaires and interviews can.

Look at change over time. Leadership development efforts often have short-term, midrange, and long-term effects. Limiting your evaluation to participants' reactions immediately after an event, or even thirty days following the event, may seem like an efficient way to quickly wrap up a study, but to accomplish most significant changes takes longer than that. There may actually be a period of reduced performance while participants are learning and practicing new skills, which is not necessarily indicative of a development initiative's failure. If your evaluation looks only at the short-term results, it may not reveal significant long-term impact or may miss the opportunity to learn how to enhance long-term and more significant impact. Design your plan to measure change at multiple, and appropriate, points in time.

Assess individual- and group-level change. Although individuals are the participants in leadership development initiatives, organizations usually expect that the development of significant numbers of individuals will have an impact at the group and/or organizational level. Restricting your assessment to individual-level change (or group-level change, for that matter) doesn't make clear the connection between individual- and group-level change. It's important to measure both kinds of change and to analyze the connections between them to understand why a development initiative did or did not have the expected impact.

Use control groups for comparison. Using control groups for comparison gives you greater certainty that the changes found in your evaluation are the result of the leadership development intervention and not of some other factor. Create your control group using people with characteristics (age, organizational level, job type, and prior training, for example) that are similar to those of the people participating in the development initiative. If the intervention is the only known systematic difference between the

Pilot Study Is a Good Evaluation Tool

A pilot study can act as a dress rehearsal for your evaluation. It can reveal unforeseen shortcomings in data-collection tools and help you hone your collection process and analysis strategies. The size of the pilot study depends on the method you're using and the type of information you're attempting to gather (Kraemer & Thiemann, 1987). If you are using assessment tools, investigate the quality of the assessments as part of the pilot (see "Reliability and Validity" on pages 37–38). Ideally, your pilot study would include an analysis of the data to determine whether the measure is properly designed to deliver the desired kind of information. The sample size of your pilot study should be similar to the intended sample size of the actual evaluation, but it should leave an adequate sample size for your formal evaluation—don't reuse pilot data.

A pilot evaluation has several benefits: you can determine whether responses seem appropriate, interview protocols can be tested to ensure that questions are clear and are eliciting intended responses, and surveys can be tested to see whether the questions are clearly written and the response options make sense.

You may not have the time, resources, or opportunity to conduct a pilot test. Another way to ensure that you will collect good information is to form a data-collection review team. This team can review any surveys or protocols you develop for use in data collection and examine the process and analysis strategies you intend to employ. Members of the team might include content matter experts (people who know about the subject area you are measuring), technical or measurement experts (people who know about measurement methods and/or research), population group experts (people familiar with the target population), and experts in the effects of bias, ethics, and similarly affective issues.

two groups and the participant group shows more change than the control group (and nothing unusual occurred during the intervention and evaluation periods), you can reasonably argue that the change resulted from the initiative.

Use time-series designs for comparison. It's often difficult to put together a control group, so another way of determining the effect of a development initiative is to gather data from the participant group well before they participate in the initiative. Then you can look at trends of growth related to the period of time before the initiative and compare them with trends that occur during and after it. As long as no other changes that may have affected the outcomes have occurred during that same time period, you can infer any differences in trends to be the result of the development initiative.

The Measurement of Change: Methods and Issues

While individuals can sometimes agree that a situation or an individual has or has not changed, they are much less likely to agree on how much change has occurred and whether the change represents an improvement. One primary cause of problems in measuring change is called *response-shift bias.* Response-shift bias occurs when individuals, having rated themselves at one time from one perspective ("I am a good leader"), change their responses at a later time, not because they see themselves as changed but because their perspectives have changed (see "Shifting Perspectives Make Measuring Individual Change Difficult" on page 36).

Evaluators who use multirater, or 360-degree, surveys to measure how a leadership development initiative has changed individual performance or behavior often use one of the following methods: pre- and post-initiative assessments, retrospective pretest and posttest assessments, and degree-of-change ratings. Each method has its own benefits and drawbacks.

Shifting Perspectives Make
Measuring Individual Change Difficult

Before participating in a leadership development initiative, managers rate themselves on a variety of questionnaires focused on leadership skills and perspectives. During the initiative, they are exposed to a variety of leadership models and to a variety of people whose perspectives about leadership differ from their own. As a result, they leave the initiative with a somewhat different idea of what effective leadership is. When they are asked after the initiative to rate their leadership skills and perspectives, it's possible that they may rate themselves the same or even lower than they rated themselves before the initiative, even though they may have actually improved in some areas they have targeted for development. This is because they are using a different definition of effectiveness than they used before the initiative or they have higher expectations for their performance. The initiative may have had impact, but the measurement of its effectiveness (using a survey in this case) may not note any change. The same effect has been found in other rater groups, such as participants' bosses, direct reports, and peers. This is especially true when survey questions are not specific enough to identify behaviors.

Pre- and post-initiative assessments. One of the most popular methods for measuring change is to use the same assessment survey before and after the leadership development initiative takes place. Some organizations may insist that a survey be readministered after an initiative has taken place because they find it too expensive to develop a new assessment survey. This technique works best in situations where what you want to measure is very specific and concrete (easily observable).

There are many factors other than the development initiative itself that could cause a change (positive or negative) in pre- and

Reliability and Validity

In general, *reliability* is the consistency of an assessment, and *validity* is the accuracy of an assessment. Neither reliability nor validity can be measured absolutely or established definitively for an assessment. Paying attention to the quality of assessment information and exploring what results mean and how they are used are important parts of the evaluation process.

Reliability is the degree to which an assessment produces consistent results. If an assessment does not produce consistent scores, you may be getting more error than information. Reliability is never truly measured, but it can be estimated. The same test will likely have different reliability estimates depending on how reliability is calculated and the sample used. The appropriate reliability level depends on the situation. Reliability is usually reported on a scale ranging from 0 to 1, with estimates closer to 1 being preferred.

There are three ways commonly used to assess reliability. *Internal consistency* provides information about whether questions on a scale are measuring the same concept. *Interrater agreement* provides information about the degree to which ratings agree. *Test-retest* provides information about the stability of questions and scales over time.

Validity is the combination of two ideas: the degree to which an assessment measures what it claims to measure and the usefulness of an assessment for a given purpose. Validity is an extremely important consideration when you are developing or using assessments. Validity is a multifaceted concept, and multiple types of evidence are needed to establish it. Evidence should be gathered in the varying situations and with the varying populations for which the assessment is intended. Validity has to do with the test, the people taking the test, the purpose of the test, and the consequences of the test.

There are several types of validity evidence. *Content validity* is the extent to which assessment adequately and comprehensively measures what it claims to measure. *Construct validity* is carried in the relationship between test content and the construct it is intended to measure. Typically, this type of evidence involves logical and/or empirical analysis, including statistical comparisons to other assessments and expert judgments of the relationship between the assessment and the construct. *Criterion validity* is found in the relationship between the assessment and a criterion such as effective performance. Consider, for example, the connection between an assessment of job performance and job performance ratings. *Concurrent evidence* refers to evidence collected at the time the test is administered, and *predictive evidence* is evidence collected at a later time.

We sometimes take for granted that an assessment is providing accurate, useful, and appropriate information. Assessments do not always do that. Validity studies are one way that question or test bias or unfairness can be revealed. *Bias* is the presence of a question or test characteristic that results in differential performance for individuals of the same ability but from different ethnic, gender, cultural, social status, or religious groups. Bias often stems from limitations of our perspective and understanding. No test is free from bias, but question and test bias and unfairness can be detected and reduced.

post-initiative assessments. Response-shift bias is one example; another is a change in the organization (restructuring, layoffs, or new compensation systems, to name a few).

Retrospective pretest and posttest assessments. Retrospective pretest and posttest assessments require two ratings at the same time after participants have completed the initiative. One rating usually focuses on describing an individual participant before the intervention. The second rating assesses the person's skills and behaviors at the time the survey is completed. The participants, their bosses, and other stakeholders can be involved in the rating process. It's beneficial to include ratings from multiple perspectives. Some evaluators doubt the merits of this method, perceiving it to create a "demand characteristic" that would automatically result in increased ratings of effectiveness from the "before" to the "now" ratings. However, CCL's research and other research in the field (Howard and others, 1979) argue for its validity. Ratings of change are highly correlated with objective measures of change such as performance appraisals.

Degree-of-change ratings. Another method for measuring change is to ask individuals to rate the degree of change using a response scale. For example, raters could select from a five-point scale ranging from "no change" to "great change." Research has shown this to be an effective method; there seems to be more agreement across rater groups (peers, direct reports, and bosses, for example) as to the amount of change when all groups are rating change directly, as compared with evaluations that measure change using pre- and posttest ratings (Peterson, 1993).

Designing the Evaluation Plan

An evaluation plan ensures that the results of a development initiative are measured so that they meet the expectations of participants, stakeholders, and the organization. Further, a plan helps stakeholders understand exactly what will be evaluated so that they can design a development initiative that will produce desired results. Organizations benefit from an evaluation plan because it lays the groundwork for improving processes and systems, thereby creating a measurable return on investment. As you plan your evaluation, be sure to indicate the relationship between specific evaluation questions, components of the leadership development initiative, timelines, and selected evaluation methods. "Evaluation Plan Design Example" on page 41 can serve as a template for a design that serves your particular circumstances.

At the time you create your evaluation plan, it's not necessary for you to have identified specific content for each method (for example, questions for your survey). Your intent at this point should be to choose methods that are likely to produce the type of data valued by key stakeholders, capable of addressing each specific evaluation question, assigned at a time that is appropriate, and used to measure the expected kind of impact. Your plan provides an overview of data-collection activities and helps ensure that you are collecting the appropriate data needed to answer the evaluation questions. For complex evaluations, you can include other activities, such as the communication of results (for example, what results are communicated, to whom, and by what media).

Choosing evaluation methods. There are many measuring techniques available to evaluators. To select the appropriate technique(s) to efficiently and effectively fulfill the purposes of the evaluation is the challenge and the goal for evaluators. In the following pages we describe several techniques that are particularly relevant to evaluating leadership development initiatives. (Examples of some of the more complex collection methods are included in this book's appendices.)

Daily evaluations. (See example in Appendix B on page 83.) In some leadership development initiatives, participants complete evaluation forms at the end of each day. The value in these forms is twofold. First, they give participants an opportunity to reflect on their daily experiences, which reinforces what they've learned. Second, they provide staff with information that enables them to make any necessary adjustments to the initiative, thereby enhancing its effectiveness. This method is somewhat limited in that it

Evaluation Plan Design Example

Evaluation Questions	Time Frame and Data-Collection Methods (Source*)			
	JAN	APR	AUG	NOV
Were learning objectives met?	Survey (P)			
How do participants intend to apply their learning and new skills?	Survey (P)			
Is there growth in competencies?		360-degree behavioral change instrument (P, M, DR, Pe, O)		
Are participants receiving support for development and application of new competencies?		Survey (P) Interviews (P)		Survey (P) Interviews (P)
What changes are resulting in participants' work groups?			Survey (P, M) Interviews (P, M)	
How is the organization benefiting?				Analysis of organizational data (C)

* Data Source Key
P = participant (individual, group, or team)   O = other (client, customer, etc.)
Pe = peer of participant   DR = direct report of participant
M = manager of participant   C = key organizational client contact

This sample plan indicates that surveys, a 360-degree assessment, interviews, and organizational data will be used in January, April, August, and November to collect data relevant to the various questions listed in the far left column. For some evaluation questions, data from multiple perspectives are gathered and multiple data-collection strategies are used. The data source key allows you to indicate where or from whom the data are being collected.

does not offer participants much time to reflect on their experiences and may not provide a comprehensive picture of the experience.

End-of-initiative evaluations. (See example in Appendix C on pages 84–87.) Participants complete end-of-initiative evaluation forms at the conclusion of each component of the leadership development initiative. You can design these forms to capture the extent to which a specific component met its target objectives, how participants intend to apply what they've learned in the workplace, and how well facilitators, facilities, and logistics met a specified standard. Use these forms to gather evidence regarding how participants intend to use lessons learned, to collect impressions of how relevant and valuable the initiative is to potential participants, and to capture suggestions for changing the initiative. Capturing this information while it is fresh on the minds of participants is helpful, but this method doesn't measure the actual implementation of the intended changes—only the intent to apply what has been learned.

Expectations and benefits comparison. (See examples in Appendices D and E on pages 88–89.) Comparing participant expectations before an initiative to their perceptions of benefits after the initiative can give you a quick reading on whether benefits measured up to or exceeded expectations. If you don't know much about the actual impact of the initiative (for example, if it's the first run of a particular initiative), the simplest way to design such a questionnaire is to develop quantitative survey questions that assess the expected objectives and then to allow some space for participants to write in other expectations they may have. From this information initiative designers and trainers can learn, before the initiative, whether participant expectations differ from initiative objectives; they can compare objectives with what participants perceive as benefits; they can see what unexpected benefits the initiative may have; and they can gain knowledge to use in redesigning the initiative and in designing change surveys for future

CCL's Approach to Evaluation Forms

Daily and final evaluation forms employ a variety of formats and rating scales. Over time, CCL has moved away from ratings of "value" and "enjoyment" to ratings of "outcome met," "knowledge gained," "application value," and "skills improved." It has also moved from rating modules or activities to rating the intended outcomes, or objectives, of leadership development initiatives. "Value" ratings are presumed to relate to "application value," and "enjoyment" ratings tell facilitators whether the individual was pleased with the experience. Each of these ratings has its place, but the leadership development field has for some time now realized that it's missing out on substantial and substantive information if it measures only "value" and "enjoyment."

Evaluation formats that use "outcome met," "knowledge gained," "application value," and "skills improved" as the target for rating scales gather more informative data. Evaluators commonly measure results against the intended outcomes of an initiative rather than the activities through which those outcomes are accomplished.

research. (See example in Appendix H on page 95 for more information about this last point.)

Interview. (See example in Appendix F on pages 90–93.) Interview questions are typically open-ended, they provide qualitative data, and they can be asked either face-to-face or by telephone. You can conduct interviews to determine the level of knowledge, skills, and attitudes gained from an individual's experience with a development initiative. You can also use interviews to assess perceptions of the initiative from a stakeholder's perspective. If resources don't allow time for one-on-one interviews, you can adapt the interview format to an open-ended questionnaire that you can mail or e-mail to participants.

Interviews are most effective when you want qualitative information to fulfill multiple purposes. Such purposes include the following:

- assisting in identifying training and learning needs, an initiative's design, or expectations for applying lessons from the development initiative (interviews would take place before the initiative),

- determining participants' reactions, experiences, and satisfaction with the initiative (interviews would take place during a longer-term initiative),

- determining participants' reactions, learning, and intentions to apply their learning (interviews would take place during an initiative or after it had ended),

- developing surveys, focus group interview questions, or the focus of an observation (interviews could take place at any point relative to an initiative, depending on the outcomes desired),

- further interpreting survey results (interviews associated with evaluation are typically most relevant for this purpose after an initiative has been completed).

Interviews have several advantages and disadvantages. One advantage is that interviews allow the evaluator to probe for clarification and deeper complexity, which results in richer data. They provide time for participants and stakeholders to reflect, which can be developmental in itself. If the evaluator conducts the interviews (as opposed to the organization's HR department, for example), acceptance and endorsement for the evaluation can increase, since participants and stakeholders often view the evaluator as an objective party. A significant disadvantage is that interviews can be more costly than other methods. If the interviews are conducted in person, for example, travel costs add to the total price of the evaluation. Interviews can also take more of the evaluator's time, both in terms of conducting the interviews and analyzing the qualitative data. Evaluators can reduce the pressure on resources by conducting phone interviews or by using Internet-based collaboration tools (such as electronic whiteboards or chat rooms), which reduce travel costs and also allow evaluators to conduct more interviews in a shorter amount of time.

Learning survey. (See example in Appendix G on page 94.) A learning survey is designed to assess the extent to which participants have learned new content during the initiative. This method is valuable when participants are expected to retain factual information (such as their organization's leadership or competency models or its business policies or practices) or learn specific steps for implementing leadership responsibilities (such as giving feedback and coaching others).

The most reliable way to assess the attainment of factual information is to administer the learning survey twice: once before the initiative and once immediately afterward. If possible, conduct a pretest before the initiative as a means of assessing the needs of participants and stakeholders; this can guide you in focusing the measures you will use in the evaluation.

The learning survey's questions should be related to the content of the initiative. To analyze the data, you can compare the responses of the two surveys. Participants may have some knowledge of the content before the initiative, and they should know most if not all of the content after the initiative ends.

Change survey. (See example in Appendix H on page 95.) Change surveys are useful in assessing whether change has occurred as a result of a development initiative. They are typically used to measure changes in attitudes or behaviors specific to the initiative in question. A well-developed change survey should be based on what is already known about the impact of the initiative and/or the objectives of the initiative. Evaluators should test survey questions for clarity and reliability in a pilot test. They should also ensure that the response scale used in the change survey facilitates the measurement of change (see "The Measurement of Change: Methods and Issues" on pages 35–39).

Change surveys are most effective when the focus of the evaluation is on behavioral changes as measured by quantitative data. Administering a change survey at different points in time has different purposes. For example, using a survey before an initiative allows the evaluator to identify behavioral shifts after an initiative so that the changes can be noted and measured. When administered several months after the initiative has ended, a change survey can be used to measure the associated behavioral change resulting from the initiative.

Valid, reliable change surveys can be time consuming to develop, but they can be relatively inexpensive to administer. They allow for responses from a large sample of people and can collect easily analyzed quantitative data. They allow for anonymity or confidentiality of responses, are useful when respondents are geographically dispersed, allow respondents to respond on their own time, and require that all respondents answer the same set of questions. On the minus side, they don't allow for changes to or clarification of questions.

Intuition can be misleading when developing a survey. Even seemingly simple choices, such as what response options to use, can have an unintended impact on results. If you plan to develop your own survey and do not have training in survey development, it is wise to seek advice from measurement or psychometric publications or from measurement professionals.

Guidelines to Writing Survey Questions

Surveys are frequently used to collect information from a large number of individuals on a broad range of subjects. Although commonly used, a survey is one of the most challenging instruments to develop well. When designed in haste, surveys often collect inaccurate and useless information.

Here are a few simple guidelines for developing survey questions. Before you begin the question-writing process, clearly identify the areas you want to assess. Select representative behaviors, skills, and competencies. Relate them to the initiative and prioritize them. Then determine the type of information you need to capture. For example, you may need to collect data related to the frequency of a specific behavior or related to the evidence that a defined skill level has been attained. This process will help you write survey questions that are specific and relevant to your evaluation.

Things to Do When Writing Survey Questions
- Be as concise as possible without losing the meaning of the question.
- Use specific language with common meaning and interpretation.
- Create several questions to measure complex phenomena.
- Write open-ended questions that ask for specific information.

Things Not to Do When Writing Survey Questions
- Don't use colloquialisms, metaphors, similes, figures of speech, culturally biased phrases, scientific words, or jargon.
- Don't be unnecessarily wordy.
- Don't use double negatives.
- Don't use inflammatory or derogatory language.
- Don't attempt to measure several ideas in a single question.

> **How CCL Measures Change**
>
> CCL typically uses a change survey called *Reflections*. This survey is designed to measure behavioral change using a "retrospective pretest and posttest" design. (This design is discussed on pages 38–39.) *Reflections* is a 360-degree follow-up assessment that provides feedback to individual participants regarding their own leadership growth and, in an aggregate form, feedback to clients and to CCL regarding the impact of an initiative on a group of participants and their organization.

A 360-degree assessment retest. Many leadership development initiatives make use of 360-degree instruments, administered before the start of the initiative, as a way of providing participants with feedback regarding the state of their leadership capabilities. To measure change, some organizations like to use the same 360-degree instrument after the initiative. Using the same instrument lets organizations get another snapshot at a particular point in time from a particular group of people and lets them compare and contrast broad themes and patterns.

Although this process seems to make sense, it does have some problems. For example, if different raters are used (which is often the case), there may be changes in scores simply because different raters are providing information. Also, participants revisiting the same 360-degree instrument will need access to someone familiar with both their original development goals and the instrument who will be available to discuss concerns and answer questions (someone like a professional coach). Scores on scales, and particularly on questions, can fluctuate even though a person's "true" score remains the same. Comparing scores (question by question or scale by scale) to measure change over time or to measure the impact of an initiative or other leadership development experience may provide misleading information. CCL's experience with 360-degree retests has demonstrated the difficulty in accurately measuring behavioral change using this method.

Behavioral observation. (See examples in Appendices I and J on pages 96–98.) Behavioral observation involves observing a set of activities, the people who are participating in those activities, and the environment in which the activities take place. Observations can produce qualitative data in the form of field notes or quantitative data if observers note their information as ratings, rankings, or frequencies.

There are several effective uses for behavioral observation. Before the initiative begins, observation can determine participants' baseline knowledge, skills or behaviors, and attitudes. During the initiative it can determine levels of interaction, engagement, skill development, and satisfaction with the initiative. Observations conducted between one week and three to six months after completion of the initiative can determine changes in knowledge, skills or behaviors, and attitudes. Behavioral observation is especially effective when it is used as one of several data-collection methods.

Compared with other evaluation methods, behavioral observation has several advantages. For example, data are collected where the activity is taking place, thus enhancing the data's validity; target activities are viewed within a context that may help interpret data collected from other methods; a trained observer might see things that others close to the initiative may miss; and the observation process can illuminate issues that interviewees are unwilling to talk about.

This evaluation method also has some limitations. It requires a well-trained observer. Multiple observers may focus on different things, thus making analysis and synthesis more difficult. Also, participants may alter their behavior if they know they are being observed. Finally, behavioral observation can be disruptive to the work environment and can be expensive if a large sample is required.

Focus groups. (See example in Appendix K on pages 99–100.) You can use a focus group interview to survey six to twelve people at one time. The primary purpose of this method is to obtain qualitative information from a group of individuals (or a team) that has had a similar experience (participation in a training program, for example). Evaluations usually make use of multiple focus group interviews and use a well-designed interview guide to focus the discussion. Focus group interviews should be carried out in a way that allows participants to feel safe disclosing information about their attitudes and perceptions regarding the initiative being evaluated. There are several excellent resources for evaluators considering using focus groups (Greenbaum, 1999; Morgan, 1993; Morgan & Krueger, 1997).

There are several ways you can use focus groups in your evaluation. Before an initiative begins, you can use focus groups to identify training or learning needs, to determine an initiative's design, or to assess expectations of how participants will apply what they learn. During an initiative (assuming the initiative takes place over several days, weeks, or months), you can use a focus group to determine participants' reactions to and experiences and satisfaction with the training initiative. After the initiative ends, you can use this evaluation method to determine participants' reactions, what they've learned, how they intend to apply their new skills and knowledge, and the relative success or challenge they've had in doing so. Focus groups are also effective when it's necessary to assess reactions, learning, and intentions of a team rather than individual participants. Some evaluators use focus groups to develop survey questions or to further interpret survey results. Another interesting product of focus groups is that they allow participants to process their experiences together, which can help them build support networks to further aid in their development.

The focus group data-collection method has several advantages. Because it captures the collective experience of individuals, interaction among participants tends to increase the number and quality of responses. It provides a forum for teams to create additional impact and meaning related to their developmental experience. It lets the interviewer probe for clarification, explanations, and examples. Participants generally enjoy being part of a focus group interview, resulting in high response rates. This method is relatively inexpensive and makes good use of time, in that it allows evaluators to collect data quickly from a large group of people.

The focus group method also has some limitations. A skilled interviewer is required to ensure that the data collected are of high quality. The interviewer has less control in a group interview than in an individual interview and so needs to have the skills and ability to keep the group on track. Data collected from a focus group may be difficult to capture and organize. Groups vary widely—some groups may develop a collective energy and provide extensive data, but other groups may lack energy and provide only superficial data.

Dialogue. (See example in Appendix L on page 101.) Group dialogue is a special kind of conversation in which people listen intently for underlying meanings and assumptions. Dialogue requires that participants suspend their assumptions in a way that enables them to hear others' perspectives objectively. This technique allows an open, creative conversation to take place, often freeing the participants in the conversation to become aware of and better understand different perspectives. Unlike a focus group, a dialogue allows the evaluator to remain relatively invisible (at his or her choosing) and to let the conversation take place between group members (McGuire & Palus, 2003).

The value in this method is that it allows team members and groups of participants to interact with each other, exploring their perspectives and insights more deeply than they might in a focus

---

Ground Rules for the Dialogue Method

The evaluative results of a dialogue session come from participants talking about their experiences in a supportive atmosphere. To achieve this goal, share these ground rules at the beginning of the session and get all participants to agree to follow them.

- Everybody has an equal place in the conversation. (It helps to sit in a circle if possible, without tables in the middle.)

- Each person says only what he or she feels comfortable saying.

- The group should agree on how the results of the dialogue will be used.

- The group should protect the confidentiality of individual remarks.

- Participants should speak to the middle of the circle and avoid one-on-one or side conversations.

- There should be a balance between advocacy (statements of belief) and inquiry (questions of clarification).

- Listen. Silence is okay. Support any quiet or solitary voices.

- Seek, surface, and explore multiple perspectives.

- Participants should work together to collaboratively understand shared experiences.

- Don't try to solve problems during the dialogue session.

- Spend time at the end for debriefing. What was good about the conversation? What was frustrating? What was learned that could be used to carry the process forward?

---

group. You can use dialogue in your evaluation to understand the different perspectives of stakeholder groups and to clarify what the collected data mean.

Measuring return on investment (ROI). Although *return on investment* is a phrase that most often refers to financial implications, it can also describe the broader impact of individual and team development initiatives on an organization. Several methods are available to evaluate such impact. Determining which is the most appropriate for a particular evaluation depends on the type of impact expected. To identify the appropriate measure at the organizational level, some useful questions to ask include the following:

- What changes at the organizational level are expected as a result of the initiative?

- Why are these changes expected? (In other words, what is the connection between the objectives of the leadership development experience and these changes?)

- When can stakeholders in the organization expect to see changes?

- Who will be able to note and report on these changes?

- How can data about these changes be obtained?

True measures of ROI include data such as the costs of facilities, trainers, materials, and the time participants spend in training and away from their jobs. ROI formulas also include the financial benefits of training, such as cost savings, new revenue, and calculations of the value of perceived job improvement. A critical step in creating accurate ROI formulas is isolating and measuring the effects of development.

Although ROI formulas work well for skills-based training and many organizations apply them to leadership development, the value of this method is limited. It doesn't provide data related to the quality of improvement. For example, an ROI of 300 percent is impressive, but without data showing where the improvement has been made, it's not possible to fully measure the impact of that improvement. To increase the validity and usefulness of ROI measurements, you can reinforce your evaluation plan with the following methods.

Workplace statistics. (For more information and a survey example, see Appendices M and N on pages 102–106.) Workplace statistics include information that organizations often gather on absenteeism, communication breakdowns, and grievances. Evaluators can obtain that information from the organization and analyze it in relation to the leadership development initiative and its objectives. Before requesting and using workplace statistics in an evaluation project, carefully determine which statistics are likely to change as a result of an individual's or team's participation in the initiative.

Workplace statistics are useful as an evaluation method when a development initiative is designed to meet specific organizational outcomes. For example, when participants are expected (as part of their action plan based on their development experience) to work differently with at-risk employees to prevent situations that might lead to grievances, it's appropriate and useful to examine the change in frequency and severity of grievances that employees file.

Workplace statistics aren't useful if there aren't links between the statistics, the expected organizational outcomes, and the development initiative. (Refer to chapter 2 to assess whether this method is an appropriate evaluation technique for your situation.)

Document analysis. Documents and records are written statements and other materials that attest to an event or provide an accounting of some activity. Evaluators who use documents typically wish to make inferences about the values, sentiments, intentions, or beliefs of the sources or authors.

Documents include letters, journals, logs, position papers, notes, speeches, newspaper articles and editorials, annual reports, newsletters, case studies, evaluation or consultants' reports, and photographs. Records are typically used to keep track of events or transactions. They might include expenditure records; expense account vouchers; financial information; performance records; professional, business, or school directories; student or participant achievement or performance test records; state or federal regulatory records; attendance records; competency or attitude score records; and electronic mail records.

This method can be effective in understanding the history or background of a program or situation; in tracking the number of times that something has occurred; in helping develop survey or interview questions or areas on which to focus an observation; in identifying patterns of participation, interest in, or attitudes toward a program; and in better understanding an issue that people are unable or unwilling to talk about.

Document analysis has several advantages as a method of data collection. Documents and records are often plentiful (stored usually in the organization's archives) and inexpensive to collect. Data from documents and records may provide useful chronological detail (possibly more accurately than a chronology built from interviews). The data gathered from documents and records are less subject to an evaluator's bias than data from interviews and observation. When used with other methods, documents and records provide a contextual richness for interpreting other data collected during the evaluation.

There are also some limitations. For example, samples of documents or records may not be representative (notes from some meetings may exist, but not from others). Personal documents may reflect a person's bias. Deliberate deception or manipulation of information is possible if the document's writer had a desire to express a certain viewpoint. Also, records may contain incomplete or out-of-date information.

Analysis of organizational systems and processes. (See example in Appendix O on page 107.) At the organizational level, one type of outcome evaluators can look for is the extent to which organizational systems and processes—aspects of the organization that directly affect employees—have been affected. Many leadership development initiatives will result in improvements to various organizational systems and processes. Initiatives that are most likely to have this effect include components that enable teams to work together more effectively, enable individuals to understand others' points of view more readily, or stimulate individuals and teams to more effective and creative problem solving and decision making. Some systems and processes for you to consider include operating procedures, educational processes, HR policies, formal and informal communication structures, financial accounting processes, and maintenance procedures.

Customer satisfaction. (See example in Appendix P on page 108.) When measuring the value of a development initiative, evaluators often find it useful to get the perspective of the customer. Although it is easy to understand this connection when the development initiative is directly related to customer service, it is not always as clear when the initiative focuses on developing individual leaders. Just how might such an initiative affect an organization's customers? Some components of effective leadership (communication and decision making, for example) have a direct effect on the relationship organizations have with customers and clients. For example, an organization whose leaders are unable or unwilling to understand what its clients need may see those clients move to a more responsive competitor.

Whether developing your own survey or interview or working with a vendor, there are several important aspects of customer service that you should investigate as a means of measuring the impact of a development initiative. They include the following:

- What type of work does the customer do with the organization? What kind of contact does a customer have with the organization (direct account service, for example, or through an independent sales force)? How frequent is the contact?

- What do customers value in their relationships with the organization?

- What do customers expect from their relationships with the organization?

- How long does it take for a customer problem to be solved or complaint to be addressed (before the development initiative compared with after the initiative), and how could the timeliness or courtesy of service be characterized?

- Can the customer describe past experiences (before the development initiative) with the organization?

- To what extent were customers satisfied with their past experiences with the organization?

- Can the customer describe current experiences (after the development initiative) with the organization?

- To what extent are customers satisfied with their current experiences with the organization?

- To what extent is the organization meeting customer expectations as the customer describes them?

Climate survey retests. When leadership development is a component in an organization's efforts to make significant improvements or changes to its work climate, it's useful to examine the extent to which that climate has changed over the course of the development initiative. This can be accomplished by making at least two assessments of the organization: one before the beginning of the initiative and one at an appropriate time after the initiative has ended. Many organizations conduct annual climate surveys as a general practice. The appropriate time to administer subsequent assessments depends on the type of climate change expected, the size and complexity of the organization, and the number of individuals who have participated in the initiative. Change in larger, more complex organizations takes more time than in less complex situations.

Organizational climate is typically defined by employees' satisfaction with specific features, such as pay and benefits, leadership, and opportunities for development. As with other measures of organizational improvement, climate change should be examined only if the leadership development initiative was designed to effect this type of large-scale change. The initiative should include a sufficient number of employees (the appropriate number depends on the type of initiative and the change desired), should be of long enough duration to create change at the organizational level, and should be designed to encourage organization-level changes.

Culture survey retests. Culture in organizations is typically defined as the behaviors and values that pervade the organization. It determines, among other things, whether a particular behavior, appropriate in one organization, is deemed inappropriate in another. The culture of an organization is built by its people and is extended through its selection, attrition, reward, and reprimand processes. Organizational culture is greater than any one individual's values or behaviors.

When leadership development is a component in an organization's efforts to make significant improvements or changes to its culture, it's useful to examine the extent to which that culture has changed over the course of the leadership development initiative. You can make this part of your evaluation by making at least two assessments of the organization: one before the beginning of the initiative and one or more at appropriate intervals after the initiative has ended. The appropriate time to administer subsequent assessments depends on the type of culture change expected, the size and complexity of the organization, and the number of individuals who have participated in the initiative. Additional administrations of assessments, including administrations during the initiative, provide stronger evidence of impact.

Culture is more embedded in the organization than is climate, and so is more difficult to change. Assessments of culture change are unlikely to reveal significant data more than once a year. As with organizational climate change, the success and speed of culture change depend largely on the size and complexity of the leadership development initiative, as well as on the position and percentage of employees involved in the initiative.

As with other measures of organizational improvement, culture change should be examined only if the leadership development initiative was designed to effect this type of large-scale change. The initiative should include an appropriate number or percentage of employees from organizational levels capable of effecting the culture change desired, should be of a duration long enough to create change at the organizational level, and should be designed to encourage organization-level changes.

Designing and Conducting the Evaluation:
A Checklist

☑ Examine impact from multiple perspectives.

☑ Assess the different kinds of change that can be observed.

☑ Use multiple data-collection methods.

☑ Look at change over time.

☑ Assess individual- and group-level change.

☑ Use control groups for comparison.

☑ Use time-series designs for comparison.

☑ If you have a large enough sample, conduct a pilot study.

☑ Consider various methods of measuring change.

☑ Be mindful of issues regarding the measurement of change.

☑ Design the evaluation plan, choosing appropriate evaluation methods.

4

USING EVALUATION FINDINGS

Evaluations often fail to live up to their full promise because what organizations learn from them goes unused. Even when organizations do put evaluation findings to use, they frequently make use of only a fraction of their potential. It's important that evaluators, individual participants, and organizations understand that the evaluation process doesn't end when all of the data have been collected, analyzed, and interpreted. On the contrary, that is the time for the organization to revisit the reasons the evaluation was originally commissioned. To ensure that your evaluation findings will be used to support individual, team, and organizational learning, be sure to complete four critical activities: effectively communicate the results, identify specific courses of action, develop a detailed action plan, and monitor the action plan's implementation.

These four activities create a greater likelihood that your evaluation's recommendations will be carefully considered and translated into action and that the actions taken based on the evaluation findings will be realistic and sensitive to the organization's culture and context. They will also help the organization identify and manage any potential barriers or obstacles to change. These activities allow those individuals affected by the changes to get involved in planning the changes. Perhaps most important, these activities lay the groundwork for the organization's using the evaluation findings as part of a continuous process of improvement and organizational learning (Preskill & Torres, 1999).

Effectively Communicate Results

Most evaluations result in a final report that is submitted to the primary stakeholder or client. All too often only a few people read that final report, so the degree of change that occurs as a result of the evaluation is limited. Evaluators can counter this tendency by carefully considering their reporting strategy while keeping the goal of a usable evaluation in mind. Organizations will more often use evaluation reports that are credible, relevant (to stakeholders' interests, expectations, and communication preferences), accurate, and fair.

One tactic to consider is the use of multiple methods for communicating and reporting the process of the evaluation and its results. A broader communication strategy can help to more widely distribute the lessons arising from development initiatives, and it also emphasizes the idea that the results of an evaluation provide information that can and should be used in an organizational learning process, that the evaluation results are not the final goal— learning is. Informing a variety of audiences about the findings of the evaluation and how the results will be used increases the credibility of the evaluation effort, communicates to stakeholders that they were heard and that the results will be acted on, and prepares stakeholders for future evaluations by demonstrating their potential value. Communication channels can include oral and multimedia presentations, executive summaries and flyers, memos, case studies, faxes, postcards, e-mail and voice mail messages, photo essays, scenarios, question-and-answer sessions, Web pages, electronic documents, newsletters, bulletins, and posters.

Beyond choosing a variety of media, you can also tailor the timing, content, and communication channel to the information you are reporting and to the stakeholder groups receiving it. To do this, take into account the stakeholder group's background, communication preferences, and information needs (much of this information should be available from the initial planning phase of the evaluation). If the information is not available, ask for it. (What information do stakeholder groups want? When do they need or want the information? How do they best receive information?)

Distributing interim reports before the release of a final report is another useful and effective communication tactic. Company executives may not have time for or interest in a complete and detailed account of findings but may benefit from an overview of results and information about the specific questions of interest to them—information that helps them make necessary changes or decisions. When a development initiative is designed to occur in stages or has separate components, evaluation reports can be issued at each stage or rolled up in a final report.

Identify Specific Courses of Action

The most useful evaluation reports provide both critical findings and recommended actions. The actions must be specific and must follow logically from the evaluation results. A good process to use in identifying specific recommendations involves four steps:

1. Based on the evaluation's results, determine what changes are needed in what areas. Broadly speaking, those changes can be to the support structure in the organization and/or to the initiative itself.

2. Examine possible revisions to the initiative and to specific areas that strengthen the organization's support structure.

3. Explore the need to follow up the leadership development initiative with another activity.

4. Gather and consult with the stakeholders.

Based on the evaluation's results, determine what changes are needed in what areas. One possible outcome of a leadership development initiative is that it has the impact stakeholders and participants have expected and hoped for. In that case, no remedial action is necessary, but the organization might want to consider its next step in the development process for its employees. Stakeholders may want to celebrate the success of the initiative.

Another possible outcome is that the data show the initiative needs to be revised to achieve maximum impact. In this case, the specific areas and suggestions for revision, based on the evaluation findings, should be identified and prioritized by relevant stakeholder groups.

Still another outcome might be that participants gain a number of new insights but aren't able to employ much of what they learn because of systemic obstacles in their work environment or a lack of understanding about how to transfer what they've learned back into their own situations. Evaluators can help identify barriers, but it's primarily the organization's responsibility to address the issues.

Depending on the nature of the obstacles, subsequent training or some other organizational development interventions may be needed. For example, if the leadership development initiative involved an organizational culture or climate survey, the information gathered from the survey may indicate the work the organization needs to do. The organization may want to update reward systems, policies, or communication processes to better reflect the vision of the organization. It may need to review and revise its leadership development agenda. Perhaps the leadership competencies being developed don't align with its business strategy or culture.

It's best if stakeholders examine these issues before the leadership development initiative, but sometimes that's not

Basic Elements of a Final Evaluation Report

A final evaluation report should be clearly written and to the point. Avoid words that may be unfamiliar to the intended audience. If you must use technical language or jargon, explain it in layperson terms. If appropriate, use graphs or narratives to illustrate a point. The report should be attractive and professional. The report's presentation should not be overwhelming; use headings and page numbers to help orient the reader. When appropriately used, color can add interest and clarity to the report. Do not skip over the most basic elements of an effective report: correct grammar, spelling, and punctuation. For organizing purposes, the following list can be a helpful guide:

Executive Summary
Purpose of the Evaluation
Description of Initiative and Sample
Caveats about the Evaluation
Overview of Processes Used and Analysis
Summary of Data (with multiple subsections)
Conclusions and Recommendations
Appendices (supporting materials)

possible. Changes in the organization or other contextual factors may occur during the initiative or may not be readily apparent before the initiative's start. It's important to maintain attention on issues of alignment throughout the initiative to best ensure its success. Organizational development experts may need to be consulted if there is a substantial incongruity among systems, processes, outcomes, and other factors.

Examine possible revisions to the initiative and to specific areas that strengthen the organization's support structure. It's possible that an evaluation's findings might indicate a need for minor or major revision to the development initiative, perhaps including additional learning needs for individuals or groups and improving specific organizational elements to support learning, thereby increasing an intervention's appeal or effect. Based on the evaluation findings, the organization may assign a group of stakeholders the task of redesigning aspects of the initiative.

Explore the need to follow up the leadership development initiative with another activity. After the results of your evaluation are in, it's a good time to explore with participants the need for follow-up developmental activities. For example, coaching may be in order for some or all of them, and some participants may benefit more from additional specific skills-based training. When an organization considers follow-up activities, it's moving toward a systems approach to leadership development, which is an improvement over single-event initiatives.

Gather and consult with the stakeholders. The most effective means for determining how to use what is learned from the evaluation is to bring together everyone with a stake in the evaluation and the initiative. This includes not just participants and stakeholders with an interest in the development initiative but also people who might be affected by changes made as a result of the findings and those individuals responsible for implementing the intended changes. The best time to do this is after you've reported evaluation results, which allows stakeholders some time to think about the results and correct any misunderstandings or errors in the report. Stakeholders should be encouraged to use data to respond to any perceived inaccuracies in the report because this creates a shared responsibility for report accuracy.

If your evaluation results illustrate the shortcomings of a specific group in particular (such as the need for participants' managers to become better development coaches for their direct reports), it may be wise to allow that group time to devise a course of action before bringing in all the stakeholders. The purpose in giving this time is to allow that specific group time to form a response and take ownership of the situation, not to put them in a defensive position.

Develop a Detailed Action Plan

Once key stakeholders have discussed potential actions, the next step for them is to develop an action plan. An action plan is a tool for implementing the lessons that result from an evaluation study. Certainly, the lessons should point to areas of leadership development initiatives that are in need of revision, and in addition, they can indicate areas (such as systems and processes) in the organization that aren't supporting those initiatives.

Not all stakeholders need to be involved in the development of the action plan, although it's often helpful to have as much involvement as possible. You can determine who needs to be involved by examining where action is needed and who has the responsibility and authority to enact change in that area. The action plan should outline specific tasks, identify individuals who are responsible for carrying them out, include necessary resources for implementing specified actions, and include a timeline for carrying them out. As a guide to creating an action-plan document, consider these questions:

- What needs to happen and why? What are the specific actions to be taken? How are the actions indicated by the evaluation results?

- Who will make it happen? What group or individual is responsible for implementing the proposed action?

- Who else need to be involved? What additional groups or individuals are needed (for example, to participate in the action, to provide approval for it, or to play a support role)?

- What barriers are anticipated? What obstacles to implementation exist? How will obstacles be addressed?

- In what order does it need to happen? Do the steps need to occur in a particular order?

- When does it need to happen? Is there a deadline for initiating and completing each step of the action plan?

- How will the stakeholders know it has happened? What indicators will be observed to determine whether each step of the action plan has been initiated and completed?

- How will success be determined? What indicators will be observed to measure the success of each step in the action plan?

Distribute the action plan that results from this effort to all those involved with the proposed actions so that all are clear about their roles in implementing the plan.

Monitor the Action Plan's Implementation

As the organization begins to implement the action plan, it's critical for progress to be monitored and communicated. Monitoring the action plan's implementation means following up with individuals and groups responsible for specific actions, as indicated in the plan, to see how well they are progressing and what, if anything, needs to be modified. One way to monitor the plan is to periodically convene the group that developed the action plan and have each member describe how well the actions are being implemented and what help is needed to continue the process. If the members of the group are geographically dispersed, you can conduct these monitoring sessions using Internet capabilities, videoconferencing systems, shared Web sites, or e-mail. Regardless of the method used, all of those involved should become aware of the extent to which the plan is being implemented and what impact the changes are having on individuals, groups, and the organization. The group might even decide that, as a result of making certain changes, additional evaluation needs have surfaced.

Using Evaluation to Create Organizational Change and Learning

Evaluation measures more than impact. The process has the potential to create change in (and for) individuals and their organizations. In addition to identifying gaps in, barriers to, and support for leadership development, evaluation can be used to help gather possible solutions and solicit ideas for improving an organization's development effort. These changes can affect the entire organization, groups of people, or individuals, depending on the type of change and the effect it has at various levels. These changes also provide an opportunity for additional evaluation and organizational learning.

Appropriate Use of Evaluation Data

The collection, storage, and use of data representing individuals should adhere to appropriate and professional standards (Joint Committee on Standards for Educational Evaluation, 1994). Following these various standards helps reduce ethical problems that can arise during the evaluation process. When you're summarizing the purpose of the evaluation in your report, it's a good idea to include a statement that any uses of the information not sanctioned by these guidelines may be misguided and erroneous because the data collected during the evaluation may not be relevant to other conclusions.

Important outcomes of evaluation include the individual and group learning that occurs as a result of participating in the evaluation and using the evaluation's results. When individuals and groups reflect upon their experiences and share what they've learned with others in the organization, the organization as a whole learns. The challenge, however, is in finding ways to capture and share this learning.

One tactic is to develop an organizational learning database that employees can access on an as-needed basis. Another tactic is to create a discussion area on the organization's intranet. Yet another is to publish, in the organization's internal newsletter and bulletins, the lessons revealed through participation in the development initiative and in the evaluation's results. Each of these methods is a vehicle for carrying information throughout the organization so employees can learn from each other—a hallmark of organizational learning. (For a list of resources related to organizational learning through evaluation, see Appendix A on pages 74–82.) In creating an evaluation plan that fosters organizational learning, it's important to consider guidelines that make the process less susceptible to misuse. Three specific issues are especially relevant to the evaluation of leadership development initiatives: maintaining confidentiality of individual data; evaluating the initiative, not the individuals; and linking the evaluation to organizational strategy.

Maintaining confidentiality of individual data builds evaluator credibility and trust that the process will be used to evaluate the initiative, not the individual. Individual data should not be shared with anyone other than that individual unless that individual gives specific permission to share the data with other specific people. Individuals (and their observers) will often be more candid and honest in their responses when they know their data will not be shared with others.

Leadership development is intended for individual, team, organizational, and community improvement. The evaluation data collected should be used to enhance the initiative itself, to foster changes in participants' leadership knowledge and skills, to encourage relevant changes in the organization and community, and to illustrate relevant factors in the organization or community related to the success of the initiative. Evaluators should encourage organizations not to use the collected data for performance appraisals or for administrative decisions regarding individual performance, since the collection of that kind of information is held to a different set of legal and professional standards (Joint Committee on Standards for Educational Evaluation, 1994). You can promote this value by aggregating any individual data collected during the evaluation to the group level.

Evaluation should be part of strategic intent. It's not intended to be a valueless exercise to which people are asked to give time, energy, and resources but which is not used for productive purposes. Just as leadership development should be linked to organizational strategy, so should evaluation be considered strategically important and be asked to contribute to the achievement of the organization's goals and its learning agenda.

Evaluation is often a complex endeavor, and it's impossible for any single book to provide all the information that may be needed for a particular situation. This brief book has provided a basic overview of the evaluative process. It has also described techniques, strategies, and guidelines that you can use to ensure that your evaluation is not an isolated process. By linking your evaluation to the design and results of development initiatives and to organizational goals, you can help organizations build systems and processes that augment the individual and group impact of leadership development. The result is an organization that can learn amid change and can adapt to remain relevant to its employees and the clients and/or customers it serves.

Using Evaluation Findings: A Checklist

☑ Write final evaluation report.

☑ Disseminate report through different media.

☑ Determine what changes are needed in what areas.

☑ Examine possible revisions to the initiative and to specific areas that strengthen the organization's support structure.

☑ Explore the need to follow up the leadership development initiative with another activity.

☑ Gather and consult with the stakeholders.

☑ Develop a detailed action plan.

☑ Monitor the action plan's implementation.

☑ Use the evaluation to create organizational change and learning.

REFERENCES

Conway, M., & Cassidy, M. F. (2000). *How to measure customer satisfaction.* Retrieved September 22, 2003, from http://store.astd.org/product.asp?prodid=179

Greenbaum, T. L. (1999). *Moderating focus groups: A practical guide for group facilitation.* Thousand Oaks, CA: Sage.

Howard, G. S., Ralph, K. M., Gulanick, N. A., Maxwell, S. E., Nance, D. W., & Gerber, S. R. (1979). Internal invalidity in pretest-posttest self-report evaluations and a re-evaluation of retrospective pretests. *Applied Psychological Measurement, 3*(1), 1–23.

Joint Committee on Standards for Educational Evaluation. (1994). *The program evaluation standards: How to assess evaluations of educational programs* (2nd ed.). Thousand Oaks, CA: Sage.

Kraemer, H. C., & Thiemann, S. (1987). *How many subjects? Statistical power analysis in research.* Thousand Oaks, CA: Sage.

McCauley, C. D., Moxley, R. S., & Van Velsor, E. (Eds.). (1998). *The Center for Creative Leadership handbook of leadership development* (1st ed.). San Francisco: Jossey-Bass.

McGuire, J. B., & Palus, C. J. (2003). Conversation piece: Using dialogue as a tool for better leadership. *Leadership in Action, 23*(1), 8–11.

Morgan, D. L. (1993). *Successful focus groups: Advancing the state of the art.* Thousand Oaks, CA: Sage.

Morgan, D. L., & Krueger, R. A. (1997). *The focus group kit* (Vols. 1–6). Thousand Oaks, CA: Sage.

Peterson, D. B. (1993). *Measuring change: A psychometric approach to evaluating individual training outcomes.* Paper presented at the eighth annual conference of the Society for Industrial and Organizational Psychology, San Francisco.

Phillips, J. J. (2000). *The consultant's scorecard.* New York: McGraw-Hill.

Preskill, H., & Torres, R. T. (1999). *Evaluative inquiry for learning in organizations.* Thousand Oaks, CA: Sage.

APPENDIX A: Evaluation Resources

This collection of resources begins with a list of publications that can often be found online or at your local public, corporate, or university library.

The second group of resources consists of e-mail and discussion groups, or listservs, for those readers who intend to join the evaluation community or would like to have access to information from other evaluators. Some listservs have searchable archives within which users can locate additional information based on their specific needs.

The third resource grouping is a list of professional organizations. These organizations often provide basic information about evaluation on their Web sites and sometimes offer channels for posting evaluation positions or proposals (for readers and users seeking evaluation services). Some of these organizations may have additional resources on their sites.

Finally, the last resource group includes Web sites with links that provide access to resources that have a great deal of useful evaluation information. The reader is advised that, as with any Web-based resource, the availability of this information can change, shift, and even disappear from the Internet without prior warning. All of the information listed here was current as of the date of this publication.

Publications

Alliger, G. M., Tannenbaum, S. I., Bennett, W., Jr., Traver, H., & Shotland, A. (1997). A meta-analysis of the relations among training criteria. *Personnel Psychology, 50*(2), 341–358.

Bassi, L. J., & Cheney, S. (1997). Benchmarking the best. *Training & Development, 51*(11), 60–64.

Bassi, L. J., & McMurrer, D. P. (1998). Training investment can mean financial performance. *Training & Development, 52*(5), 40–43.

Beywl, W., & Potter, P. (1998). RENOMO—a design tool for evaluations. *Evaluation, 4*(1), 53–71.

Brinkerhof, R. O. (2003). *The success case method: Find out quickly what's working and what's not.* San Francisco: Berrett-Koehler Publishers.

Brown, S. M., & Seidner, C. J. (Eds.). (1998). *Evaluating corporate training: Models and issues.* Boston: Kluwer Academic Publishers.

Brunner, I., & Guzman, A. (1989). Participatory evaluation: A tool to assess projects and empower people. *New Directions in Program Evaluation, 42,* 9–17.

Carter, L., Giber, D., & Goldsmith, M. (Eds.). (2001). *Best practices in organization development and change: Culture, leadership, retention, performance, coaching.* San Francisco: Jossey-Bass.

Chelimsky, E., & Shadish, W. R. (1997). *Evaluation for the 21st century: A handbook.* Thousand Oaks, CA: Sage.

Chen, H. (1990). *Theory-driven evaluations.* Thousand Oaks, CA: Sage.

Church, A. H., & Waclawski, J. (2001). *Designing and using organizational surveys: A seven-step process.* San Francisco: Jossey-Bass.

Coomber, R. (1997). Using the Internet for survey research. *Sociological Research Online, 2*(2). Retrieved from http://www.socresonline.org.uk/socresonline/2/2/2.html

Cousins, J. B., & Earl, L. M. (1992). The case for participatory evaluation. *Educational Evaluation and Policy Analysis, 14*(4), 397–418.

Dainty, P., & Lucas, D. (1992). Clarifying the confusion: A practical framework for evaluating outdoor development programmes for managers. *Management Education and Development, 23*(2), 106–122.

Davidson, J. (in press). *The multipurpose evaluation guidebook: The nuts and bolts of putting together a solid evaluation.* Thousand Oaks, CA: Sage.

Dixon, N. M. (1987, August). Meet training's goals without reaction forms. *Personnel Journal, 66*(8), 108–115.

Edwards, J. E., Scott, J. C., & Nambury, S. R. (2003). *The human resources program-evaluation handbook.* Thousand Oaks, CA: Sage.

Finison, K., & Szedlak, F. (1997). General Motors does a needs analysis. *Training & Development, 51*(5), 103–104.

Fishel, B. (1998). A new perspective: How to get the real story from attitude surveys. *Training, 35*(2), 91–94.

Fitz-Gibbon, C. T., & Morris, L. L. (1987). *How to design a program evaluation.* Thousand Oaks, CA: Sage.

Fitzpatrick, J. L., Worthen, B. R., & Sanders, J. R. (2003). *Program evaluation: Alternative approaches and practical guidelines* (3rd ed.). New York: Longman.

Forss, K., & Carlsson, J. (1997). The quest for quality—or can evaluation findings be trusted? *Evaluation, 3*(4), 481–501.

Forss, K., Cracknell, B., & Samset, K. (1994). Can evaluation help an organization to learn? *Evaluation Review, 18*(5), 574–591.

Greene, J. G. (1988). Stakeholder participation and utilization in program evaluation. *Evaluation Review, 12*(2), 91–116.

Hackett, B. (1997, December). The value of training in the era of intellectual capital. *The Conference Board* (Report No. 1199-97-RR).

Henerson, M. E., Morris, L. L., & Fitz-Gibbon, C. T. (1987). *How to measure attitudes.* Thousand Oaks, CA: Sage.

Herman, J. L., Morris, L. L., & Fitz-Gibbon, C. T. (1987). *Evaluator's handbook.* Thousand Oaks, CA: Sage.

Insch, G. S., Moore, J. E., & Murphy, L. D. (1997). Content analysis in leadership research: Examples, procedures, and suggestions for future use. *Leadership Quarterly, 8*(1), 1–25.

Jenlink, P. M. (1994). Using evaluation to understand the learning architecture of an organization. *Evaluation and Program Planning, 17*(3), 315–325.

Julian, D. (1997). The utilization of the logic model as a system level planning and evaluation device. *Evaluation and Program Planning, 20*(3), 251–257.

Kaplan, R. S., & Norton, D. P. (1992, January–February). The balanced scorecard—measures that drive performance. *Harvard Business Review,* pp. 71–79.

Kaplan, R. S., & Norton, D. P. (1993, September–October). Putting the balanced scorecard to work. *Harvard Business Review*, pp. 134–147.

Kaplan, R. S., & Norton, D. P. (1996). *The balanced scorecard.* Boston: Harvard Business School Press.

King, J. A., Morris, L. L., & Fitz-Gibbon, C. T. (1987). *How to assess program implementation.* Thousand Oaks, CA: Sage.

Kirkpatrick, D. L. (1998). *Another look at evaluating training programs.* Alexandria, VA: American Society for Training and Development.

Kirkpatrick, D. L. (1998). *Evaluating training programs: The four levels* (2nd ed.). San Francisco: Berrett-Koehler.

Krueger, R. A. (1994). *Focus groups: A practical guide for applied research.* Thousand Oaks, CA: Sage.

Martineau, J. (1998). Using 360-degree surveys to assess change. In W. Tornow & M. London (Eds.), *Maximizing the value of 360-degree feedback: A process for individual and organizational development* (pp. 217–248). San Francisco: Jossey-Bass.

McCauley, C. D., & Van Velsor, E. (Eds.). (2004). *The Center for Creative Leadership handbook of leadership development* (2nd ed.). San Francisco: Jossey-Bass.

McEvoy, G. M., & Buller, P. F. (1990). Five uneasy pieces in the training evaluation puzzle. *Training & Development, 44*(8), 39–42.

Miner, N. J. (1998). Anonymous evaluations ain't what they used to be! *Training & Development, 52*(3), 12–14.

Mohr, L. B. (1995). *Impact analysis for program evaluation.* Thousand Oaks, CA: Sage.

Monnier, E. (1997). Vertical partnerships: The opportunities and constraints which they pose for high quality evaluations. *Evaluation, 3*(1), 110–118.

Morris, L. L., Fitz-Gibbon, C. T., & Freeman, M. E. (1987). *How to communicate evaluation findings.* Thousand Oaks, CA: Sage.

Morris, L. L., Fitz-Gibbon, C. T., & Lindheim, E. (1987). *How to measure performance and use tests.* Thousand Oaks, CA: Sage.

Munck, M. E. (1997). Bridging the macro and micro levels in outcome evaluation. *Evaluation, 3*(3), 320–344.

Murphy, J. R. (1997). Results first, change second. *Training, 34*(5), 58–67.

Owen, J. M., & Lambert, F. C. (1995). Roles for evaluation in learning organizations. *Evaluation, 1*(2), 237–250.

Palus, C. J., & Horth, D. M. (2002). *The leader's edge: Six creative competencies for navigating complex challenges.* San Francisco: Jossey-Bass.

Patton, M. Q. (1987). *How to use qualitative methods in evaluation.* Thousand Oaks, CA: Sage.

Patton, M. Q. (1994). Developmental evaluation. *Evaluation Practice, 15*(3), 311–319.

Patton, M. Q. (1997). *Utilization-focused evaluation.* Thousand Oaks, CA: Sage.

Peterson, R. A. (2000). *Constructing effective questionnaires.* Thousand Oaks, CA: Sage.

Phillips, A. D. (1990). Taking a good look at development. *Issues & Observations, 10*(3), 1–5.

Phillips, J. J. (1983). *Handbook of training evaluation and measurement methods.* Houston, TX: Gulf Publishing Company.

Phillips, J. J. (1994). *Measuring return on investment* (Vols. 1–2). Alexandria, VA: American Society for Training and Development.

Phillips, J. J. (1996). How much is the training worth? *Training & Development, 50*(4), 20–24.

Phillips, J. J. (1997). *Return on investment in training and performance improvement programs.* Houston, TX: Gulf Publishing Company.

Preskill, H. (1994). Evaluation's role in enhancing organizational learning: A model for practice. *Evaluation and Program Planning, 17*(3), 291–297.

Preskill, H. (1997). *HRD evaluation as the catalyst for organizational learning.* Paper presented at the annual meeting of the Academy of Human Resource Development, Atlanta, GA.

Preskill, H., & Torres, R. T. (1999). Building capacity for organizational learning through evaluative inquiry. *Evaluation, 5*(1), 42–60.

Rogers, P., Hacsi, T., Petrosino, A., & Huebner, T. (Eds.). (2000). Program theory in evaluation: Challenges and opportunities. *New Directions for Evaluation, 87,* 1–115.

Schwandt, T. A. (1997). Evaluation as practical hermeneutics. *Evaluation, 3*(1), 69–83.

Scriven, M. (1996). The theory behind practical evaluation. *Evaluation, 2*(4), 393–404.

Shadish, W. R., Cook, T. D., & Leviton, L. C. (1995). *Foundations of program evaluation: Theories of practice.* Thousand Oaks, CA: Sage.

Smith, A. (1993). Management development evaluation and effectiveness. *Journal of Management Development, 12*(1), 20–32.

Smith, M. E., & Brandenburg, D. C. (1991). Summative evaluation. *Performance Improvement Quarterly, 4*(2), 35–58.

Sonnichsen, R. C. (2000). *High impact internal evaluation: A practitioner's guide to evaluating and consulting inside organizations.* Thousand Oaks, CA: Sage.

Stake, R. E. (1995). *The art of case study research.* Thousand Oaks, CA: Sage.

Stecher, B. M., & Davis, W. A. (1987). *How to focus an evaluation.* Thousand Oaks, CA: Sage.

Torres, R. T. (1994). Concluding remarks: Evaluation and learning organizations: Where do we go from here? *Evaluation and Program Planning, 17*(3), 339–340.

Torres, R. T., Preskill, H. S., & Piontek, M. E. (1996). *Evaluation strategies for communicating and reporting: Enhancing learning in organizations.* Thousand Oaks, CA: Sage.

Torres, R. T., Preskill, H. S., & Piontek, M. E. (1997). Communicating and reporting practices and concerns of internal and external evaluators. *Evaluation Practice, 18*(2), 105–125.

Van Velsor, E. (1998). Assessing the impact of development experiences. In C. D. McCauley, R. S. Moxley, & E. Van Velsor (Eds.), *The Center for Creative Leadership handbook of leadership development* (pp. 262–288). San Francisco: Jossey-Bass.

Wholey, J. S., Hatry, H. P., & Newcomer, K. E. (1994). *Handbook of practical program evaluation.* San Francisco: Jossey-Bass.

Willyerd, K. A. (1997, March). Balancing your evaluation act. *Training, 34*(3), 52–58.

Yin, R. (1984). *Case study research: Design and methods.* Beverly Hills, CA: Sage.

Zahn, D. (1998). Lessons from the front, back, and sides of the room. *Training & Development, 52*(1), 12–13.

Electronic Mail and Discussion Groups

EVALTALK. This group was established to provide a vehicle for open discussions concerning evaluation issues. Although it is sponsored by the American Evaluation Association (AEA), the list is available for anyone to use. To subscribe to EVALTALK, send e-mail to LISTSERV@UA1VM.UA.EDU. The body of the message should read: SUBSCRIBE EVALTALK FirstName LastName

GOVTEVAL. This forum houses a discussion of government program evaluation. To subscribe to GOVTEVAL, send e-mail to MAJORDOMO@NAIONET.NET. The body of the message should read: SUBSCRIBE GOVTEVAL [your e-mail address].

National Professional Organizations

ACADEMY OF HUMAN RESOURCE
   DEVELOPMENT
College of Technology
Bowling Green State University
Bowling Green, OH 43403
Phone: (419) 372-9155
http://www.ahrd.org/

ACADEMY OF MANAGEMENT
P. O. Box 3020
Briarcliff Manor, NY 10510-
   8020
Phone: (914) 923-2607
http://apps.aomonline.org/
   MemberDirectory/main.asp

AMERICAN EDUCATIONAL
RESEARCH ASSOCIATION
1230 17th Street, NW
Washington, DC 20036-3078
Phone: (202) 223-9485
http://www.aera.net

AMERICAN EVALUATION
ASSOCIATION
16 Sconticut Neck Road, #290
Fairhaven, MA 02719
Phone: (888) 232-2275
http://www.eval.org

AMERICAN MANAGEMENT
ASSOCIATION INTERNATIONAL
1601 Broadway
New York, NY 10019
Phone: (212) 586-8100
http://www.amanet.org

AMERICAN PSYCHOLOGICAL
ASSOCIATION
750 First Street, NE
Washington, DC 20002-4242
Phone: (800) 374-2721,
  (202) 336-5510
http://www.apa.org

AMERICAN PSYCHOLOGICAL
SOCIETY
1010 Vermont Avenue, NW,
  Suite 1100
Washington, DC 20005-4907
Phone: (202) 783-2077
http://
  www.psychologicalscience.org

AMERICAN SOCIETY FOR TRAINING
AND DEVELOPMENT
1640 King Street, Box 1443
Alexandria, VA 22313-2043
Phone: (703) 683-8100
http://www.astd.org

AUSTRALASIAN EVALUATION
SOCIETY
Victoria University of
  Technology
P. O. Box 14428
Melbourne City, MC VIC 8001
Phone: 03 9248 1315
http://www.aes.asn.au

CANADIAN EVALUATION SOCIETY
La Société Canadienne
  d'Evaluation
1485 Laperriere Avenue
Ottawa, ON K1Z 7S8
Phone: (613) 725-2526
http://
  consultation.evaluationcanada.ca

INTERNATIONAL SOCIETY FOR
PERFORMANCE IMPROVEMENT
1400 Spring Street, Suite 260
Silver Spring, MD 20910
Phone: (301) 587-8570
http://www.ispi.org

NATIONAL COUNCIL FOR
MEASUREMENT IN EDUCATION
Central Office
1230 17th Street, NW
Washington, DC 20036-3078
Phone: (202) 223-9318
http://www.ncme.org

PSYCHOMETRIC SOCIETY
207 Curry Building
P. O. Box 26171
University of NC at Greensboro
Greensboro, NC 27402-6171
Phone: (336) 334-3474
http://
  www.psychometricsociety.org

SOCIETY FOR APPLIED SOCIOLOGY
Social Research Associates, Inc.
5638 Glen Avenue
Minnetonka, MN 55345
Phone: (952) 974-0892
http://www.appliedsoc.org

SOCIETY FOR HUMAN RESOURCE
  MANAGEMENT
1800 Duke Street
Alexandria, VA 22314
Phone: (703) 548-3440
http://www.shrm.org

SOCIETY FOR INDUSTRIAL AND
  ORGANIZATIONAL PSYCHOLOGY
SIOP Administrative Office
P. O. Box 87
Bowling Green, OH 43402
Phone: (419) 353-0032
http://www.siop.org

Web Sites with Evaluation Links

Electronic Resources for Evaluators
www.luc.edu/faculty/eposava/resource.htm

Educational Resources Information Center Clearinghouse on
  Assessment and Evaluation
http://www.ericae.net/

The Evaluation Center at Western Michigan University
http://www.wmich.edu/evalctr/pubs/ecpub.htm

The Free Management Library
http://www.mapnp.org/library/

SocioNet Evaluation Links
http://www.socio.com/

W. F. Kellogg Foundation
http://www.wkkf.org/

APPENDIX B: Daily Evaluation Form (Example)

The daily evaluation process is designed to provide reflection for you and to provide the staff with feedback about this development initiative. Your candid responses are important and appreciated, especially your additional written comments.

Today's Experience

	Low				High
Please rate the day in terms of its learning value.	1	2	3	4	5
Please rate the day in terms of its job relevance.	1	2	3	4	5

What was your most beneficial learning today? Why?

_____

_____

How might you use your understanding of coaching skills in developing, teaching, and coaching others?

_____

_____

_____

_____

What additional information would have been helpful?

_____

_____

Is there anything else we should know about your experience today?

_____

_____

APPENDIX C: End-of-Initiative Evaluation Form (Example)

In addition to gathering information about the impact of the development initiative, evaluators often need to measure participant satisfaction with third-party services. Those services might include assistance given prior to the initiative, the facilities used during the initiative, food and beverage services, hotel services, and transportation. If any of these or other services are employed during the course of the development initiative, you can add sections to this example.

Final Evaluation

Please complete this evaluation form to provide us with helpful feedback on your experience.

Your Name (optional): _____

Outcomes

To what extent has each of the following outcomes been met? Also, please indicate to what extent each outcome is applicable to your specific work situation. Please use the following scale:

1 = *Not at all*	2 = To a *little* extent	3 = To *some* extent	4 = To a *great* extent	5 = To a *very great* extent

Outcome	Outcome Met?		How Applicable?	
This initiative has enabled me to . . .	*Not at all* ─ *Very great*		*Not at all* ─ *Very great*	
1. Understand the purpose of organizational and individual core values.	1 2 3 4 5		1 2 3 4 5	
2. Identify my core values and relate them to the core values of my organization.	1 2 3 4 5		1 2 3 4 5	
3. Create a personal mission statement.	1 2 3 4 5		1 2 3 4 5	
4. Identify my leadership strengths and weaknesses.	1 2 3 4 5		1 2 3 4 5	
5. Value differences between myself and others.	1 2 3 4 5		1 2 3 4 5	
6. Create a plan to strengthen my professional network.	1 2 3 4 5		1 2 3 4 5	
7. Deliver feedback effectively.	1 2 3 4 5		1 2 3 4 5	
8. Use feedback I receive from others to increase my effectiveness.	1 2 3 4 5		1 2 3 4 5	
9. Collaborate effectively with my colleagues.	1 2 3 4 5		1 2 3 4 5	

Facilitator Impact

Please evaluate each facilitator's ability to create an effective learning environment based on the following criteria: Content Knowledge, Group Facilitation Skill, and Overall Effectiveness.

Facilitators' Names	Content Knowledge				
	Very little				*Very great*
_____	1	2	3	4	5
_____	1	2	3	4	5
_____	1	2	3	4	5
_____	1	2	3	4	5

Facilitators' Names	Group Facilitation Skill				
	Very little				*Very great*
_____	1	2	3	4	5
_____	1	2	3	4	5
_____	1	2	3	4	5
_____	1	2	3	4	5

Facilitators' Names	Overall Effectiveness				
	Very little				*Very great*
_____	1	2	3	4	5
_____	1	2	3	4	5
_____	1	2	3	4	5
_____	1	2	3	4	5

Comments. What did you find particularly effective or helpful about your facilitators? (Please comment on other staff, if appropriate.)

Comments. What do your facilitators need to improve? (Please comment on other staff, if appropriate.)

Overall Initiative

	Very little			Very great	
Please rate your *overall satisfaction* with the initiative.	1	2	3	4	5

Comments. Please comment on any aspect of the initiative that you found particularly helpful.

Comments. Please comment on any aspect of the initiative that you would like to see changed.

Personal Impact. How have you benefited from your participation in this initiative?

Organizational Impact. What changes do you anticipate that your group, business unit, or organization will experience as a result of your participation?

APPENDIX D: Preinitiative Expectations Survey (Example)

To what extent does each of these developmental areas represent a goal on which you want to work during this leadership development initiative? Use the scale below for your ratings.

Not at all		To some extent		To a great extent
1	2	3	4	5

___ Improve Self-Awareness
- learn how others perceive you
- understand how your management style impacts those with whom you work
- be aware of the impact of your behavior on others

___ Improve Self-Confidence
- be self-assured
- believe you can make valuable contributions to the organization
- recognize and appreciate your talents and abilities

___ Build and Maintain Relationships
- be approachable and receptive to others
- support and understand the needs of others
- display patience with others in difficult situations
- avoid being abrasive with others

___ Work across Organizational Boundaries
- consider the impact of your actions on the entire system
- balance what is good for the unit or area with the needs of other parts of the organization
- deal effectively with contradictory requirements or inconsistencies in the organization
- evaluate the organization in a clear and objective manner

[And so on, until all objectives have been addressed.]

APPENDIX E: Post-Initiative Benefits Survey (Example)

Using the scale below, please indicate (by writing in the appropriate number to the left of the item) the extent to which you see each of the areas as an area of benefit for you personally. Where do you believe the impact of this initiative lies for you?

Not at all		To some extent		To a great extent
1	2	3	4	5

____ Improve Self-Awareness
- learn how others perceive you
- understand how your management style impacts those with whom you work
- be aware of the impact of your behavior on others

____ Improve Self-Confidence
- be self-assured
- believe you can make valuable contributions to the organization
- recognize and appreciate your talents and abilities

____ Build and Maintain Relationships
- be approachable and receptive to others
- support and understand the needs of others
- display patience with others in difficult situations
- avoid being abrasive with others

____ Work across Organizational Boundaries
- consider the impact of your actions on the entire system
- balance what is good for the unit or area with the needs of other parts of the organization
- deal effectively with contradictory requirements or inconsistencies in the organization
- evaluate the organization in a clear and objective manner

[And so on, until all objectives have been addressed.]

APPENDIX F: Individual Interview (Example)

In this example, scripted speech that the interviewer can use, except for the question examples, appears in italics. Directions for the evaluator or interviewer appear in italics and are enclosed in brackets.

Program Name: _____

Interviewer Name: _____

Interviewee Name: _____

Interview Date: _____

We like to check in with people about thirty days after an initiative to see how they are doing with their goals and development plans. Is this a good time to talk? From time to time we do an extended interview to learn more about the long-term impact of leadership development and to measure the support and the obstacles to implementing development plans on the job. Your responses are confidential. The interview will take about thirty minutes. I'd like to start by having you tell me a little bit about your experience in the initiative.

Why did you attend the initiative?

What were you looking for?

Did you get what you were looking for?

What stands out for you at this point with respect to lessons or insights you may have had?

Do any of the activities you did during the initiative stand out for you as you think back on them? Why?

Have you continued any of the activities, such as *[list activities]*?

What was the initiative's most valuable activity to you?

Did you take an issue to the initiative?

What was that issue?

Why did you pick that issue?

Did any new or different issues come up during the initiative?

Did your issue change?

Did you make any progress on your issue(s) during the initiative?

How did you work on these issues?

Can you tell me a little about your goals and/or development plan created at the end of the initiative?

In what ways have you been successful in implementing your development plan?

How do you know you have been successful?

What has helped you make progress?

Was there any impact on your organization?

Describe any incidents that reflect what you learned in the initiative.

Have you applied anything from the initiative to your work?

What happened?

What was the result?

Have you applied anything from the initiative to your life outside of work?

What happened?

What was the result?

[Probe for details here. Keep probing for specific examples of events, behaviors, experiments they did, results, and impacts. Nonwork as well as work experiences are germane. Get them to be specific. Try to understand their story and ask questions to clarify your understanding.]

What obstacles have you encountered?

In what ways, if any, are you dissatisfied with your progress?

What kinds of support have you been able to put in place for your ongoing development? For example, if you did a preinitiative interview with someone in your company, did you follow that up with a discussion about your development plan?

How has that been helpful?

Do you believe your leadership behaviors or capacities have changed as a result of this initiative?

If so, how?

Have you changed your behavior as a result of the initiative?

Can you give examples of those changes?

Can you describe what is different about you?

What do you do now that you didn't or couldn't do before?

Do you think others perceive these changes?

How do you think others would describe these changes?

Is your team changing because of any influences from the initiative?

Do you interact differently with peers, your boss, or your direct reports?

Are you more effective or less effective because of something you learned in the initiative? Provide some specific examples.

Is your organization changing because of any influences from the initiative?

Do you find support for, or resistance to, change? Provide some examples.

Have you experienced any change in the way you see your role as a leader or in the way you understand the leadership challenges you face as a result of your experience in this initiative?

Do you have any sense of what kinds of follow-up activities might be useful for you over the next year or two?

Can you describe any doubts or skepticism you had along the way about the content of the initiative? Did you have those doubts before, during, or after the initiative?

What happened to the doubts?

What kinds of thoughts and feelings did you have right after the initiative, when you finished the program and went back home?

Do you remember any of your experiences from that period?

Do you have any other thoughts about the initiative and its meaning to you?

Have you recommended this initiative to anyone else? If so, why did you recommend the initiative to them?

APPENDIX G: Learning Survey (Example)

Potential Learning Survey Questions

What are the eight competencies necessary for leadership success in ABC Organization (list all eight)?

What are the primary ways in which leaders fail at ABC Organization?

What are the primary components of the "Success for Leadership" model?

How are ABC Organization's competencies related to the "Success for Leadership" model (draw a diagram)?

What are the key steps in an effective decision-making process?

What are the key steps in the "Coaching Others" process?

What activities are leaders expected to implement as part of ABC Organization's succession-planning process?

What is the chain of command for decisions related to new-project initiation at ABC Organization?

Which groups are leadership teams at ABC Organization expected to include in decisions related to performance improvement and measurement practices?

APPENDIX H: Change Survey (Example)

Using the rating scale provided below, please indicate (by writing in the appropriate number to the left of the item) the extent to which you have changed in the indicated areas.

1 = considerable change for the worse
2 = moderate change for the worse
3 = a little change for the worse
4 = no change
5 = a little change for the better
6 = moderate change for the better
7 = considerable change for the better

____ Improved Self-Awareness
- learn how others perceive you
- understand how your management style impacts those with whom you work
- be aware of the impact of your behavior on others

____ Improved Self-Confidence
- be self-assured
- believe you can make valuable contributions to the organization
- recognize and appreciate your talents and abilities

____ Building and Maintaining Relationships
- be approachable and receptive to others
- support and understand the needs of others
- display patience with others in difficult situations
- avoid being abrasive with others

____ Working across Organizational Boundaries
- consider the impact of your actions on the entire system
- balance what is good for the unit or area with the needs of other parts of the organization
- deal effectively with contradictory requirements or inconsistencies in the organization
- evaluate the organization in a clear and objective manner

[And so on, until all objectives have been addressed.]

APPENDIX I: Behavioral Observation: Qualitative Data (Example)

In this example, directions for the evaluator or interviewer are followed by possible responses, which appear in italics. In these directions, *participant* refers to the individual who has attended the development initiative being evaluated.

Describe behaviors that indicate that the participant is accepting feedback from others.

Pat listened as Fred explained that her behaviors made him feel uncomfortable in the meeting.

Pat thanked Fred for the feedback and told him how she would try to change those particular behaviors in the future.

Pat asked Fred to continue to feel comfortable in sharing his feedback with her.

Describe behaviors that indicate that the participant is effectively delivering feedback to others.

Pat told Mary that her presentation was well received by the client but needed to be tightened for the next presentation.

Pat gave Mary suggestions for tightening her presentation.

Pat made herself available to Mary for future questions.

Describe behaviors that indicate that the participant is making effective decisions.

Pat involved three key stakeholders in the decision about the new product.

Pat listened to input from the stakeholders, each of whom had a differing opinion.

Pat overtly weighed the stakeholders' opinions in making her final decision.

Describe behaviors that indicate that the participant is working effectively across organizational boundaries.

Pat negotiated with the materials development director regarding a new product.

Pat and the materials development director worked together to resolve the issue.

Pat and the materials development director together presented the solution to senior management.

APPENDIX J: Behavioral Observation: Quantitative Data (Example)

In this example, behavioral descriptions are followed by possible responses.

Behavioral Observation Rating Table

Behavior	Time of occurrence (specify).	With whom (provide name).	Was it effective (yes or no)?
Accepted feedback from others.	10:35 a.m. 1:15 p.m.	Fred Joan	Yes No
Provided feedback to others.	2:15 p.m.	Mary	Yes
Showed confidence when speaking.	10:35 a.m.	Fred	Yes
Recognized others' performance.	2:15 p.m.	Mary	Yes
Gave constructive criticism to others.	1:15 p.m.	Joan	Yes
Delegated authority to others.	9:25 a.m.	Pete	No
Influenced others (peers).	Not observed		

APPENDIX K: Focus Group Interview Questions (Example)

In this example, questions are classified by the type of information they provide. During the design of your own evaluation, you may want to use questions more specific to your situation and organizational context. To gain the broadest possible perspective, balance the types of information you seek through your interview.

Interview Question	Type of Information
One at a time, tell us your name and something about what you learned from the leadership development initiative.	Learning, team awareness change
What are the most serious challenges facing your team at the current time?	Learning, team awareness change
Talk about how the initiative addressed these challenges.	Satisfaction
Were you satisfied with what you learned in this initiative? Why or why not?	Satisfaction
Do you believe that this initiative will enable your team to meet its challenges more effectively? If so, how? If not, what is missing?	Satisfaction
Suppose your organization wanted your team's input on whether it should continue offering this development initiative for its leaders. What would you say?	Satisfaction
What goal(s) for improvement did your team set as a result of the initiative?	Behavior change

Interview Question	Type of Information
What has your team accomplished relative to its goal(s)?	Behavior change
What challenges has your team encountered in attempting to work on its goal(s)?	Behavior change
How has your team attempted to overcome these challenges or barriers to goal accomplishment?	Behavior change
What have your team members learned about each other as a result of this initiative?	Learning, team awareness change
How will this new learning have an impact on the work of the team?	Learning, team awareness change
What suggestions for improvement do you have for the sponsors and designers of this initiative?	Satisfaction

APPENDIX L: Group Dialogue Questions (Example)

A group dialogue often requires little intervention by the evaluator. However, it may be necessary during the dialogue for evaluators to refocus the conversation on the topic at hand. Below are listed some sample questions to seed and focus a dialogue. Each question is followed by a description of the type of information that it potentially makes available (satisfaction, learning, and/or behavioral change). During the design of your own evaluation, you may want to use questions more specific to your situation and the organizational context. To gain the broadest possible perspective, balance the types of information you seek through dialogue.

Dialogue Question	Potential Information
What stands out for you when you think about the experience of the initiative itself?	Satisfaction, learning
What stands out for you when you think about the impacts of the initiative?	Learning, behavioral change
What can you do now that you couldn't or didn't do before the initiative?	Behavioral change
What's the value of the initiative experience?	Satisfaction, learning, behavioral change
What do you see as the impact on other people? On the team as a whole?	Behavioral change
What could be done differently to improve the initiative?	Satisfaction
Are we missing anything in our dialogue so far?	Satisfaction

APPENDIX M: Workplace Statistics (List of Measures)

Evaluators can collect and measure data in the following categories as a method for determining return on investment from a development initiative (adapted from Phillips, 2000).

Hard Data

Output
- Units produced
- Tons manufactured
- Items assembled
- Items sold

Sales
- Forms processed
- Loans approved
- Patients visited
- Applications processed
- Students graduated
- Tasks completed
- Productivity
- Work backlog
- Incentive bonus
- Shipments
- New accounts generated

Time
- Cycle time
- Response time for complaint
- Equipment downtime
- Overtime
- Average delay time
- Time to project completion
- Processing time
- Supervisory time
- Training time
- Meeting time
- Repair time
- Efficiency (time based)
- Work stoppages
- Order response time
- Late reporting
- Lost time or days

Costs
- Budget variances
- Unit costs
- Cost by account
- Variable costs
- Fixed costs
- Overhead costs
- Delay costs
- Penalties or fines
- Project cost savings
- Accident costs
- Program costs
- Sales expense
- Administrative costs
- Average cost reduction

Quality
- Scrap
- Waste
- Rejects
- Error rates
- Rework
- Shortages
- Product defects
- Deviation from standard
- Product failures
- Inventory adjustments
- Percentage of tasks completed properly
- Number of accidents
- Customer complaints

Soft Data

Work Habits
Absenteeism
Tardiness
Visits to the dispensary
First aid treatments
Violations of safety rules
Number of communication
  breakdowns
Excessive breaks
Customer Service
Customer complaints
Customer satisfaction
Customer dissatisfaction
Customer impressions
Customer loyalty
Customer retention
Customer value
Lost customers
Work Climate, Satisfaction
Number of grievances
Number of discrimination
  charges
Employee complaints
Litigation
Job satisfaction
Organizational commitment
Employee turnover
Attitude shifts
Employee loyalty
Increased confidence

Employee Development
Number of promotions
Number of pay increases
Number of training programs
  attended
Requests for transfer
Performance appraisal ratings
Increases in job effectiveness
Innovation
Implementation of new ideas
Successful completion of
  projects
Number of suggestions
  implemented
Setting goals and objectives
New products and services
  developed
New patents and copyrights

APPENDIX N: Workplace Statistics Survey (Example)

The following survey was developed as a means of assessing self- and manager-reported evidence of return on investment resulting from a leadership development initiative.

Business Outcomes

Please provide a numeric rating for each of the outcomes listed below or indicate NR if the outcome is not relevant to your situation.

My own development and improved leadership effectiveness have contributed to organizational change as expressed below:

	Decreased dramatically	Decreased	Not changed	Increased	Increased dramatically	Not relevant
1. Productivity within the group I lead has . . .	1	2	3	4	5	NR
2. Profit within the group I lead has . . .	1	2	3	4	5	NR
3. Level of trust and collaboration within the group I lead has . . .	1	2	3	4	5	NR
4. Customer satisfaction with the group I lead has . . .	1	2	3	4	5	NR
5. Customer loyalty to the group I lead has . . .	1	2	3	4	5	NR
6. Employee job satisfaction among my subordinate group has . . .	1	2	3	4	5	NR

	Decreased dramatically	Decreased	Not changed	Increased	Increased dramatically	Not relevant
7. Employee promotions among my subordinate group have . . .	1	2	3	4	5	NR
8. The number of training programs attended by employees in my group has . . .	1	2	3	4	5	NR
9. Employee job effectiveness among my subordinate group has . . .	1	2	3	4	5	NR
10. Innovation within the group I lead has . . .	1	2	3	4	5	NR
11. Implementation of new ideas within the group I lead has . . .	1	2	3	4	5	NR
12. Successful completion of projects within the group I lead has . . .	1	2	3	4	5	NR
13. New products and services developed within the group I lead have . . .	1	2	3	4	5	NR

Please note that in the preceding items, higher scores are preferred. In the items that follow, lower scores are preferred.

	Decreased dramatically	Decreased	Not changed	Increased	Increased dramatically	Not relevant
14. Absenteeism among my subordinate group has . . .	1	2	3	4	5	NR
15. Tardiness among my subordinate group has . . .	1	2	3	4	5	NR
16. Employee turnover among my subordinate group has . . .	1	2	3	4	5	NR
17. Requests for employee transfers among my subordinate group have . . .	1	2	3	4	5	NR

Provide quantitative evidence for the two areas (above) that have shown the most impact (for example, the percent of increased employee promotions among your subordinate group or money saved because of a particular change you've implemented).

APPENDIX O: Measuring Change in Organizational Systems and Processes

Assess changes in systems that are related to leadership development. For example, if participants in a leadership development initiative are expected to influence an organization's decision-making processes related to hiring practices, HR policies should be examined. Following are sample questions to ask:

Did HR policies need to change?

If so, how have they changed?

Are the changes in line with what you would have expected?

If not, how are they different?

What has been the result of the change?

What evidence can the organization produce to show an impact from the change in its HR policies?

APPENDIX P: Measuring Customer Satisfaction

ASTD's Info-line titled "How to Measure Customer Satisfaction" (Conway & Cassidy, 2000) provides numerous examples for measuring customer satisfaction through the use of interviews and surveys. Among these are the following:

Overall Satisfaction Questions
How well did Acme, Inc., meet your expectations on a scale from "did not meet my expectations" to "exceeded my expectations"?

Comparative Questions
Compared to customer service from vendors other than Acme, Acme's customer service is which of the following:

- much better than I expected
- better than I expected
- about what I expected
- somewhat less than I expected
- much less than I expected

Behavioral Intention Questions
How likely is it that you will switch your business from Acme to another provider in the next six months?

- extremely likely
- very likely
- somewhat likely
- about a 50-50 chance
- somewhat unlikely
- very unlikely
- extremely unlikely

SELECTED CCL PUBLICATIONS

GUIDEBOOKS

SOURCEBOOKS

Emerging Leaders: An Annotated Bibliography (2001, Stock #352) $20.00

Executive Coaching: An Annotated Bibliography (2000, Stock #347) $20.00

Geographically Dispersed Teams: An Annotated Bibliography (1999, Stock #346) $20.00

High-Performance Work Organizations: Definitions, Practices, and an Annotated Bibliography (1999, Stock #342) $20.00

Leadership Resources: A Guide to Training and Development Tools (8th Edition) (2000, Stock #348) $49.95

Management Development Through Job Experiences: An Annotated Bibliography (1998, Stock #337) $10.00

Perspectives on Dialogue: Making Talk Developmental for Individuals and Organizations (1996, Stock #168) $20.00

Selecting International Executives: A Suggested Framework and Annotated Bibliography (1999, Stock #345) $20.00

Selection at the Top: An Annotated Bibliography (1997, Stock #333) $20.00

Succession Planning: An Annotated Bibliography and Summary of Commonly Reported Organizational Practices (1995, Stock #324) $10.00

The Human Side of Knowledge Management: An Annotated Bibliography (2000, Stock #349) $20.00

Visual Explorer: Picturing Approaches to Complex Challenges (2001, Stock #395) $395.00

Workforce Reductions: An Annotated Bibliography (1999, Stock #344) .. $20.00

FIELDBOOKS

Crisis Leadership (2003, Stock #185) $20.00

Eighty-eight Assignments for Development in Place (1989, Stock #136) .. $15.00

Evaluating the Impact of Leadership Development: A Professional Guide (2004, Stock #187) $25.00

Four Essential Ways That Coaching Can Help Executives (1997, Stock #175) $10.00

Internalizing Strengths: An Overlooked Way of Overcoming Weaknesses in Managers (1999, Stock #182) $15.00

International Success: Selecting, Developing, and Supporting Expatriate Managers (1998, Stock #180) $15.00

Managing Across Cultures: A Learning Framework (1996, Stock #173) ... $15.00

Preventing Derailment: What To Do Before It's Too Late (1989, Stock #138) $25.00

FYI For Your Improvement: Coaching and Development Guide
(3rd Edition) (2002, Stock #336) $70.00
Healing the Wounds: Overcoming the Trauma of Layoffs and
Revitalizing Downsized Organizations (1993, Stock #245) $34.00
High Flyers: Developing the Next Generation of Leaders (1997,
Stock #293) $29.95
If I'm In Charge Here, Why Is Everybody Laughing? (1984, Stock #205) $12.95
If You Don't Know Where You're Going, You'll Probably End Up
Somewhere Else (1974, Stock #203) $12.95
Inside View: A Leader's Observations on Leadership (1997, Stock #176) ... $6.00
Leadership: Enhancing the Lessons of Experience (4th Edition) (2002,
Stock #266B) $92.50
Leadership for Turbulent Times (1995, Stock #325) $7.50
Losing Your Job—Reclaiming Your Soul: Stories of Resilience,
Renewal, and Hope (1997, Stock #292) $28.95
Making Common Sense: Leadership as Meaning-making in a
Community of Practice (1994, Stock #156) $15.00
Relax, It's Only Uncertainty: Lead the Way When the Way Is Changing
(2001, Stock #2112) $27.00
The Complete Inklings: Columns on Leadership and Creativity (1999,
Stock #343) $20.00
The Intuitive Principal: A Guide to Leadership (2000, Stock #2070) $20.95
The Lessons of Experience: How Successful Executives Develop on the
Job (1988, Stock #211) $28.00
The New Leaders: Leadership Diversity in America (1988, Stock #238A) $19.95
Why Managers Have Trouble Empowering: A Theoretical Perspective
Based on Concepts of Adult Development (1993, Stock #155) $7.50

JOSSEY-BASS/CCL ALLIANCE PUBLICATIONS

Discovering the Leader in You: A Guide to Realizing Your Personal
Leadership Potential (2001, Stock #2067) $34.00
Executive Selection: Strategies for Success (2000, Stock #2057) $38.00
Leadership and Spirit: Breathing New Vitality and Energy into
Individuals and Organizations (1999, Stock #2035) $36.00
Leading in Black and White: Working Across the Racial Divide in
Corporate America (2003, Stock #2126) $27.95
Maximizing the Value of 360-degree Feedback: A Process for Successful
Individual and Organizational Development (1998, Stock #295) $45.00

Positive Turbulence: Developing Climates for Creativity, Innovation, and Renewal (1999, Stock #2031) $35.00

Standing at the Crossroads: Next Steps for High-Achieving Women (2002, Stock #2117) $26.95

Success for the New Global Manager: How to Work Across Distances, Countries, and Cultures (2002, Stock #2111) $29.95

The Center for Creative Leadership Handbook of Leadership Development (Second Edition) (2004, Stock #2150) $85.00

The Deep Blue Sea: Rethinking the Source of Leadership (2001, Stock #2068) $27.95

The Leader's Edge: Six Creative Competencies for Navigating Complex Challenges (2002, Stock #2116) $29.95

PACKAGES

Conflict Guidebook Package (Stock #731; includes 416, 418, 419) $19.95

Feedback Guidebook Package (Stock #724; includes 400, 403, 405) $19.95

Development Guidebook Package (Stock #726; includes 401, 404, 409, 411) $29.95

ORDERING INFORMATION

To order publications, please contact us at **336 545 2810** or visit our online bookstore at **www.ccl.org/publications**. The Center accepts American Express, Discover, MasterCard, Visa, and personal check. Only orders over $100 can be invoiced. Prepayment is required for all orders under $100.

Federal I.D. #23-707-9591.

Discounts are available. To receive a complete catalog, call **336 545 2810**, or e-mail **info@leaders.ccl.org**.

All prices are subject to change.